RECORD-BREAKING COMPREHENSION

YEAR 5

Gill Howell

Published by

in association with

Rising Stars UK Ltd.
7 Hatchers Mews, Bermondsey Street, London, SE1 3GS
www.risingstars-uk.com

Every effort has been made to trace copyright holders and obtain their permission for the use of copyright materials. The author and publisher will gladly receive information enabling them to rectify any error or omission in subsequent editions. All facts are correct at time of going to press. All referenced websites were correct at the time this book went to press.

Text, design and layout © Rising Stars UK Ltd.
The right of Gill Howell to be identified as the author of this work has been asserted by her in accordance with the Copyright, Design and Patents Act 1998.

Published 2013

Published in association with Guinness World Records.

Author: Gill Howell
Text design: Burville-Riley Partnership/Fakenham Prepress Solutions
Logo design: Words & Pictures Ltd
Typesetting: Fakenham Prepress Solutions
Cover design: Burville-Riley Partnership
Publisher: Becca Law
Project manager: Tracey Cowell
Editor: Jennie Clifford

Photo acknowledgements
Page 12: © Kazuhiko Yoshino/iStockphoto; **page 18**: © airn/iStockphoto; **page 24**: courtesy of fuzzimo; **page 36**: © Julien Tromeur/iStockphoto; **page 38**: © Andres Rodriguez/iStockphoto; **page 50**: © aarrows/iStockphoto. **Rising Stars is grateful to Guinness World Records for supplying all of the record-related pictures in the book.**

All rights reserved. No part of this publication may be reproduced, stored in a retrieval system, or transmitted, in any form by any means, electronic, mechanical, photocopying, recording or otherwise, without the prior permission of Rising Stars.

British Library Cataloguing in Publication Data.
A CIP record for this book is available from the British Library.

ISBN: 978-0-85769-565-9

Printed by Craft Print International Limited, Singapore

CONTENTS

How to use this book	4
Reading comprehension	6
Reading between the lines	7
Most pairs in a three-legged race	8
Longest career as a weather forecaster	10
Largest bhangra dance	12
Most guide dogs trained by an organisation	14
Farthest distance limbo-skating under cars	16
Youngest male to row an ocean solo	18
Hottest chilli	20
Most skateboard nollies in 30 seconds	22
Largest hands	24
Fastest talker	26
Tallest teenager living (male)	28
Largest vertical garden (green wall)	30
Largest hairy family	32
Heaviest vehicle pulled by hair (female)	34
Largest gathering of people dressed as leprechauns	36
Most decks of playing cards memorised – single sighting	38
Largest torchlit parade	40
Longest fingernails (female) – ever	42
Shortest living woman	44
Largest drumming lesson	46
Deepest scuba dive in sea water	48
Strangest diet	50
Largest gymnastic display (female)	52
Largest atlas	54
Reading skills	56

HOW TO USE THIS BOOK

Record-Breaking Comprehension features some of the most fascinating, weird and wonderful records from the Guinness World Records archive.

In this book, you will:

- read the exciting record-breaking stories
- practise and improve your comprehension skills
- go beyond the record to find out more.

The text

Each record or topic is described using a fiction or non-fiction text type, including newspaper reports, instructional web pages, blog entries and letters.

RECORD-BREAKING COMPREHENSION

MOST PAIRS IN A THREE-LEGGED RACE

VILLAGE FUN DAY

Saturday 28 July from 11.30 am

Once again, our volunteers have been preparing for the annual Village Fun Day.

This year's festivities will include:

★ live music from The Marshland Muckers
★ a display from the Owl Sanctuary
★ skittles
★ archery
★ performances from the Penny School of Dancing.

There will be food stalls, including a barbecue and tea tent organised by the Women's Institute.

All ages will be catered for.

The Main Event
At 2.00 pm the three-legged race will start. We want as many of you to enter as possible. Let's break the village record for the most pairs of competitors! There is no age limit, so boys and girls, mums and dads, grannies and granddads, fill in the entry form below, tie up your trainers and get ready for a good time!

Tear off the form below the dotted line and take it to the Village Hall before Friday 20 July.

Fun Fact
Did you know that the largest three-legged race in the world had 551 pairs of runners? It was held at Morecambe Community High School in Lancashire on 23 March 2012.

That's more people than live in our entire village!

Three-Legged Race Entry Form

Runner 1
Name: _____
Age: _____
Address: _____

Telephone: _____

Runner 2
Name: _____
Age: _____
Address: _____

Telephone: _____

Questions

Answer the questions to help you practise and improve your reading comprehension skills.

For help on answering questions, see pages 6–7.

The questions cover a range of different reading skills. For more information on these skills, see page 56.

Most pairs in a three-legged race

ON YOUR MARKS

a. On what date will the Village Fun Day be held?
b. What would you see at the Owl Sanctuary display?
c. Why do the organisers want lots of people to enter the three-legged race?
d. Why does the entry form have space for two entrants?

GET SET

a. What have the volunteers been doing?
b. Has the village held a three-legged race before? How do you know?
c. Why aren't the organisers trying to break the Guinness World Record?
d. What phrase is used to persuade people to enter the race?

GO FOR GOLD!

a. How many pairs of runners took part in the largest three-legged race in the world?
b. Why is there no age limit for entrants to the three-legged race in the village?
c. What does 'all ages will be catered for' mean?
d. Give two purposes of the flier.

Beyond the record

In this section you will be asked to find out more about a record or topic and present your findings. This might be by using books or the internet.

BEYOND THE RECORD

Imagine you are organising a School Fun Day. What sort of activities and events will you have? Write five questions for a questionnaire to find out which activities would be the most popular with the children in your class.

9

READING COMPREHENSION

Reading the text

Read the text carefully. Don't rush. Try to immerse yourself in the information and enjoy it.

When you have finished, take a moment to reflect and think about what you have read. What was the author's purpose? Did the text make sense? Was there anything you didn't understand?

The questions

Always read the questions carefully before you begin to write. Then you will understand what you are being asked to do.

The questions check that you can:

- make sense of what you are reading
- find information and ideas in the text
- work out what the author means
- understand why a text is organised in a particular way
- comment on vocabulary and style
- say how a text makes you feel
- link what you read to your own life.

Answering the questions

Read the instructions carefully before you start to answer, as they give you information about how to answer the questions. Don't rush your answer.

Remember to refer to the text. You do not need to answer any questions from memory.

READING BETWEEN THE LINES

An author doesn't always tell you exactly what is happening. He or she often gives you clues to help you work it out for yourself.

Read the text below and then look at the worked question examples underneath.

> Woofs and wags abounded at the annual Summer Fair. There were 15 entrants who competed for the Toss and Fetch Cup. This was won by Andy May and Buster. Buster caught one disc as many times as Andy could throw it in 60 seconds. He gained extra points by making several mid-air catches and was awarded a respectable 9.5 points.
>
> Another duo, Misty and Olivia, hope to go on to international competitions.
>
> 'We are practising hard to get Misty holding more discs and want to try for the Guinness World Record,' said proud owner Olivia.

a. How many entrants were in the competition?

The answer can be found in the text itself – 15.

b. What or who is Buster?

The text doesn't actually say, but from reading the clues ('Woofs and wags', 'Toss and Fetch Cup') it becomes clear that Buster is a dog.

c. How did Misty's owner feel about her dog's success?

Again, the text doesn't actually say, but you can draw your own conclusion from the text: '"We are practising hard to get Misty holding more discs and want to try for the Guinness World Record," said proud owner Olivia' implies that Olivia is very pleased with Misty's success.

RECORD-BREAKING COMPREHENSION

MOST PAIRS IN A THREE-LEGGED RACE

VILLAGE FUN DAY

Saturday 28 July from 11.30 am

Once again, our volunteers have been preparing for the annual Village Fun Day.

This year's festivities will include:
- ★ live music from The Marshland Muckers
- ★ a display from the Owl Sanctuary
- ★ skittles
- ★ archery
- ★ performances from the Penny School of Dancing.

The Main Event
At 2.00 pm the three-legged race will start. We want as many of you to enter as possible. Let's break the village record for the most pairs of competitors! There is no age limit, so boys and girls, mums and dads, grannies and granddads, fill in the entry form below, tie up your trainers and get ready for a good time!

Tear off the form below the dotted line and take it to the Village Hall before Friday 20 July.

There will be food stalls, including a barbecue and tea tent organised by the Women's Institute.

All ages will be catered for.

Fun Fact
Did you know that the largest three-legged race in the world had 551 pairs of runners? It was held at Morecambe Community High School in Lancashire on 23 March 2012.

That's more people than live in our entire village!

Three-Legged Race Entry Form

Runner 1
Name: _____
Age: _____
Address: _____
_____
Telephone: _____

Runner 2
Name: _____
Age: _____
Address: _____
_____
Telephone: _____

Most pairs in a three-legged race

YR 5

ON YOUR MARKS

a. On what date will the Village Fun Day be held?
b. What would you see at the Owl Sanctuary display?
c. Why do the organisers want lots of people to enter the three-legged race?
d. Why does the entry form have space for two entrants?

GET SET

a. What have the volunteers been doing?
b. Has the village held a three-legged race before? How do you know?
c. Why aren't the organisers trying to break the Guinness World Record?
d. What phrase is used to persuade people to enter the race?

GO FOR GOLD!

a. How many pairs of runners took part in the largest three-legged race in the world?
b. Why is there no age limit for entrants to the three-legged race in the village?
c. What does 'all ages will be catered for' mean?
d. Give two purposes of the flier.

BEYOND THE RECORD

Imagine you are organising a School Fun Day. What sort of activities and events will you have? Write five questions for a questionnaire to find out which activities would be the most popular with the children in your class.

9

RECORD-BREAKING COMPREHENSION

LONGEST CAREER AS A WEATHER FORECASTER

www.weatherfacts/DaveDevall

Weather for Kidz

Weather facts

Knowing what the weather will be like over the next few days helps us plan what to do, what to wear and where to go. The weather forecast is extremely important for sailors and pilots, who need reliable information about wind speed. Farmers need to know how the weather might affect their livestock and harvests.

When weather forecasters make mistakes . . .

In 1987, a TV weather forecaster predicted that a hurricane was *not* on its way. A day later, the worst storm in living memory struck the south of Britain. People were not prepared and at least 13 people died. The weather forecaster has never been allowed to forget his mistake!

In April 2009, weather forecasters told everyone to prepare for a 'barbecue summer'. What followed was heavy rain, cold and cloudy conditions, and severe flooding.

How long might a weather forecaster's career last if he or she kept getting it wrong?

Longest career as a weather forecaster

One weather forecaster who must have been popular with his viewers was Dave Devall of CTV Toronto, in Ontario, Canada. He presented the weather forecast for 48 years, 2 months, 27 days. His career began on 7 January 1961 and lasted until he retired on 3 April 2009. This earned him the Guinness World Record for the longest career as a weather forecaster. He can't have got it wrong too often!

- Weather today
- Long range
- Cloud types
- **Weather facts**
- Measuring weather
- Contact

Longest career as a weather forecaster   YR 5

ON YOUR MARKS

a. In what year did the worst storm in living memory strike Britain?
b. Why is the weather forecast important for sailors?
c. Was 2009 a 'barbecue summer'? How do you know?
d. Why do you think weather forecasters sometimes make mistakes?

GET SET

a. What part of Britain was hit by the 1987 storm?
b. How do you think the weather forecast helps farmers?
c. Why hasn't the weather forecaster from 1987 been allowed to forget his mistake?
d. What does the word 'reliable' mean?

GO FOR GOLD!

a. In which city was Dave Devall a TV weather forecaster?
b. When are forecasters unpopular?
c. Why is 'not' in the second paragraph written in italics?
d. Why do you think Dave Devall 'can't have got it wrong too often'?

BEYOND THE RECORD

Watch one weather forecast every day for a week and write down what the weather is like each day. At the end of the week, compare each forecast with the actual weather for that day. How accurate were each of the weather forecasts?

RECORD-BREAKING COMPREHENSION
LARGEST BHANGRA DANCE

12 November 2010

I love bhangra! It's lively and colourful and *so* much fun.

I am staying with my aunty and uncle in India and got the surprise *of my life* yesterday. A Guinness World Record attempt for the largest bhangra dance was held in a local town and I got to go. I cannot believe my luck!

My uncle is a lecturer at the Punjab Agricultural University in Ludhiana, where the record attempt was hosted. I begged him to take me and, unbelievably, he managed to get three tickets!

Aunty, Uncle and I all went together. It was really crowded and hot when we got there. We were sitting at the back and I thought I wouldn't be able to see anything. I wasn't too bothered initially as someone from The Art of Living Foundation, who organised it, was giving a speech.

When the dancing started, Aunty let me stand on my chair. That made all the difference. I could see all 2,100 dancers, who were dressed in the brightest colours, and dancing in time with the music, which was incredibly loud! The atmosphere was electric!

We found out after the performance that the dancers had achieved the record, so it was fabulous for everybody, not just me.

I'll never forget the experience!

Largest bhangra dance

YR 5

ON YOUR MARKS

a. Who was the author staying with in India?
b. What was the author's impression of the dancing?
c. What helped her uncle find out about the record attempt?
d. Why did the author beg her uncle to take her?

GET SET

a. Who organised the record attempt?
b. What did the author mean when she wrote 'The atmosphere was electric!'?
c. How did the author feel before the dancing started?
d. Why did the author say it was 'fabulous for everybody'?

GO FOR GOLD!

a. Which two adjectives does the author use to describe the room where the record attempt took place?
b. Which words and phrases in the text tell you this is an informal recount?
c. How did the author's feelings change during the event?
d. How is this text similar to other recounts that you have read?

BEYOND THE RECORD

Bhangra is a type of folk dance from India. Use the internet to find out about other kinds of traditional dance from five countries around the world.

13

RECORD-BREAKING COMPREHENSION
MOST GUIDE DOGS TRAINED BY AN ORGANISATION

COULD YOU BE A PUPPY WALKER?

Volunteers play a vital role as Puppy Walkers at the Guide Dogs for the Blind Association (GDBA).

Young puppies are demanding and need a lot of time, commitment and love. As a Puppy Walker, you will help to produce a very special dog, who is invaluable to a blind or partially sighted person.

As of 2006, GDBA successfully trained 26,019 dogs to provide mobility assistance to blind and partially sighted people. GDBA is a charity that was founded in 1934. It is the largest assistance-dog organisation in the world.

Could you:
- give a puppy '(from six weeks until one-year old) a loving home?
- familiarise the puppy with busy streets, shops, public transport and car travel?
- help the puppy learn to behave calmly with people, children and other animals?
- teach the puppy to be responsive to his/her handler and well behaved on the lead?

If you are able do all this, you could be the person GDBA needs!

You won't be left to fend for yourself or thrown in at the deep end! GDBA Puppy Walker Supervisors will support you through all stages of the process.

You will also be introduced to other volunteers in the puppy-walking community and make new friends.

You could make a difference.

Contact the Guide Dogs for the Blind Association for more information and to apply.

Most guide dogs trained by an organisation YR 5

ON YOUR MARKS

a. What does the Guide Dogs for the Blind Association do?
b. Why would a Puppy Walker need lots of time, commitment and love?
c. What kind of text is this?
d. What does the phrase 'thrown in at the deep end' mean?

GET SET

a. How long does a Puppy Walker keep a puppy for?
b. What is the author trying to get the reader to do?
c. Why do you think volunteer Puppy Walkers play a vital role?
d. Why does the text say 'You could make a difference'?

GO FOR GOLD!

a. Who supports Puppy Walkers through the process?
b. What are the rewards of being a Puppy Walker?
c. What does 'mobility assistance' mean?
d. Why does the text ask the reader questions?

BEYOND THE RECORD

What do you think the best and worst aspects of being a Puppy Walker might be? Write a balanced argument giving the pros and cons.

RECORD-BREAKING COMPREHENSION

FARTHEST DISTANCE LIMBO-SKATING UNDER CARS

The Daily Mumbai News — Thursday 17 February 2011

ROLLING INTO THE RECORD BOOKS

Young Rohan Ajit Kokane astonished onlookers at the Juhu Aerodrome today when he skated into the record books.

Dressed in green lycra and sporting a purple headband, Rohan achieved the farthest distance limbo-skating under cars record by gliding under 20 cars for an extraordinary distance of 38.68 m.

Rohan set off some distance away from the line of cars and built up speed before bending down parallel to the ground. Doing the splits, and with his hands on his feet, he rolled underneath the line of cars through a gap of only 35 cm.

For 30 seconds, onlookers held their breath as Rohan rolled beneath the tunnel of cars. When he emerged and heard that he had achieved a Guinness World Record, he jumped for joy.

Rohan, from Belgaum in the south of India, has been skating for four-and-a-half years. He practises for four hours a day to make sure he stays flexible and controlled. He began skating using just one skate because it was all his family could afford to buy him.

All limbo-skating fans can see Rohan's amazing feat on the TV show, *Ab India Todega*, later this week.

by **SONIA SAHIL**

Farthest distance limbo-skating under cars

YR 5

ON YOUR MARKS

a. On what date did Rohan achieve the Guinness World Record for limbo-skating?
b. Why did Rohan set off some distance away from the line of cars?
c. What features tell us this is a newspaper article?
d. Why do you think the onlookers held their breath?

GET SET

a. How far did Rohan limbo-skate?
b. Why did Rohan need to build up speed?
c. Why did Rohan jump for joy?
d. In what way is being flexible important for limbo-skating?

GO FOR GOLD!

a. How high was the gap under the line of cars?
b. How does Rohan stay flexible?
c. What does 'emerged' mean?
d. How do you think Rohan felt about having only one skate?

BEYOND THE RECORD

Imagine you are a television news reporter covering the record attempt. Write a short script for your broadcast, using the information in the newspaper report. What powerful adjectives will you use to keep your viewers interested?

RECORD-BREAKING COMPREHENSION

YOUNGEST MALE TO ROW AN OCEAN SOLO

All at Sea

Oliver Hicks became the youngest male rower to cross an ocean alone and unsupported when he rowed across the Atlantic Ocean between 27 May and 28 September 2005. He was 23 years, 175 days when he set off. He rowed from Atlantic Highlands, New Jersey, USA, to St Mary's in the Scilly Isles, UK. It took him 123 days, 22 hours, 8 minutes in his boat *Miss Olive, Virgin Atlantic*.

Crossing an ocean or sea in a ship is usually very safe. Crossing the Atlantic Ocean alone in a rowing boat, without any support, is a very dangerous activity for a number of reasons.

FLOATING CONTAINERS
Half-submerged plastic containers are a hazard if you hit them.

FALLING OVERBOARD
If you are rowing solo on the ocean and fall overboard, the chance of being rescued is very slim.

WHALES
Whales can be very dangerous if they swim too close to a small boat. They can cause a swell that swamps the boat, or can dive underwater and upturn the boat.

FREAK WAVES
Pressure waves from underwater volcanic eruptions can generate gigantic waves in an otherwise calm sea.

FREIGHTERS
It is difficult to judge the distance of a boat at night. You can be hit by a freighter because the crew on board have not spotted your craft.

WEATHER
You might encounter storms or even hurricanes. The waves in the Atlantic Ocean can be huge.

Heroes and Adventurers

Youngest male to row an ocean solo

YR 5

ON YOUR MARKS

a. What is the chance of being rescued if you fall overboard when you are rowing solo?
b. Why might the crew on a freighter not spot a rowing boat?
c. What does 'rowing solo' mean?
d. Why might a freak wave be dangerous?

GET SET

a. What might happen when a whale comes too near a boat?
b. What do you think the purpose of this text is?
c. Why is it difficult to judge the distance of a boat at night?
d. What might happen if you hit a plastic container?

GO FOR GOLD!

a. What results from an underwater volcanic eruption?
b. What word in the text means 'danger'?
c. In what two ways can waves be dangerous for a rowing boat?
d. Why do you think Oliver Hicks wasn't deterred by the dangers of the Atlantic?

BEYOND THE RECORD

What equipment do you think would be essential for a journey like this? Write a kit list for a long-distance rowing journey.

19

RECORD-BREAKING COMPREHENSION

HOTTEST CHILLI

CHILLIES

Growing chillies

Growing hot Habanero chillies is simple. Follow these easy steps.

1. Fill a seed tray with compost.
2. Place the chilli seeds 5 cm apart on the compost.
3. Cover the seeds lightly with compost.
4. Water the seeds gently.
5. Cover the seed tray with cling film and place in a warm place, such as an airing cupboard. Water the seeds regularly.
6. After two-to-four weeks, when the seedlings have appeared, move the tray to a warm, light place. Do not allow the compost to dry out.
7. When the seedlings sprout a second pair of leaves, transplant them into individual pots. Feed the plants every week with tomato food.
8. When the plants reach 30 cm in height, pinch out the tip to encourage bushiness.
9. Snip off the first chillies when they are still green. This encourages more chillies to grow. Let the next chillies turn red.

Can you take the heat?

- Red chillies are hotter than green chillies.
- The hottest chilli in the world, as of 1 March 2011, is the Trinidad Scorpion 'Butch T', which was grown by The Chilli Factory in Australia. This was tested and rated at 1,463,700 Scoville Heat Units (SHU) according to tests conducted by EML Consulting Services in Morisset, New South Wales, Australia. Cayenne pepper only scores up to 50,000 in the Scoville Heat Test!

98 HOW TO GARDEN

Hottest chilli YR 5

 ## ON YOUR MARKS

a. How far apart should you plant the chilli seeds?
b. Why should you water the seeds 'gently'?
c. Why should you let the chillies turn red?
d. Why should you feed the plants with tomato food?

 ## GET SET

a. What should you do when the seedlings appear?
b. What should you do to stop the compost drying out?
c. Why does the author use the 'Can you take the heat?' sub-heading?
d. Why is the order of the instructions important?

 ## GO FOR GOLD!

a. Why should you snip off the first chillies?
b. Why do you think the seed tray should be covered with cling film?
c. How does the world's hottest chilli compare to cayenne pepper?
d. What in this text is similar to, or different from, other texts you have read?

 ## BEYOND THE RECORD

Chillies are used in cooking to make food taste spicy or hot. Find 10 recipes that contain chillies and create a chart to grade the spiciness of each recipe.

21

RECORD-BREAKING COMPREHENSION

MOST SKATEBOARD NOLLIES IN 30 SECONDS

Skateboarding skills

Do you know your ollies from your nollies? Try these simple tricks that are bound to get you hooked on skateboarding!

As you try out different tricks, you are bound to fall off your skateboard. Don't let this put you off! Wear knee pads, elbow pads and a helmet to help stop you getting hurt.

The more you practise, the more tricks you'll be able to land.

 The Hippy Jump
As you approach a rail, jump over it, leaving your board to roll underneath. Land on your board on the other side of the rail.

 The Ollie
This is the most important trick to learn as it is the basis for several other tricks. Place one foot at the back of the board and the other midway along it. Bend your knees, then press down the tail of the board with your back foot. As it begins to flick up, lift your other foot up and slide it up towards the nose of the board. Both you and the board should leave the ground. Lift off!

 The Nollie
This is a variation of the ollie in which you flick up the nose of the board instead of the back. The name literally means a 'nose ollie'.

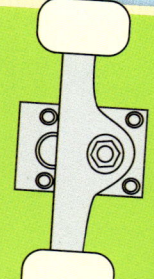 The Guinness World Record for the most nollies in 30 seconds is 15. Ivan Sebastian Cordova (USA) achieved this at X Games 15 in Los Angeles, California on 1 August 2009.

 **The Pop Shove It**
This is a really impressive trick. It starts off as an ollie, but then you kick the board so it spins 180 degrees before you land back on it.

6 *Sundaze for Kids*

Most skateboard nollies in 30 seconds   YR 5

ON YOUR MARKS

a. What is the name of the trick in which you jump over a rail?
b. What does the phrase 'hooked on' mean?
c. Why would practising help you land more tricks?
d. Which trick do you think would be easiest? Why?

GET SET

a. What is the record number of nollies in 30 seconds?
b. On average, how long did it take Ivan Sebastian Cordova to do a single nollie?
c. What feature is used in the text to highlight safety information about skateboarding?
d. Which trick do you think would be the most difficult? Why?

GO FOR GOLD!

a. How does the nollie differ from the ollie?
b. Where does the name 'nollie' come from?
c. Why has the author written parts of this text in the present tense?
d. What might go wrong when you try out a new trick?

BEYOND THE RECORD

Find out more about one of the tricks in the text. Use this information to write a short script for the presenter of a skateboarding 'how to' video.

23

RECORD-BREAKING COMPREHENSION

LARGEST HANDS

Remember to wash your hands!

Many bacteria are harmless, but others can cause colds, flu and upset stomachs. The most common way that bacteria are spread is by people not washing their hands properly (or at all!) and then transferring bacteria onto objects that other people touch. You can help stop the spread of bacterial infection by washing your hands properly.

When should you wash your hands?

You should wash your hands:
- before you prepare food
- before you eat food
- before looking after a cut or graze
- after you use the toilet
- after you handle an animal
- after you play in the garden.

How should you wash your hands?

1. Wet your hands with warm water.
2. Cover your hands with soap or handwash.
3. Rub your palms together. Rub each palm over the back of the other hand.
4. Spread your fingers on both hands and interlock them. Rub in between them.
5. Rub each thumb with the palms of your hands.
6. Rinse both hands with water.
7. Dry your hands thoroughly. Using a hand-drier machine is more hygienic than using a towel.

The whole process should take at least 15 seconds.

Did you know …?

The length of an average adult hand is 18.9 cm for men and 17.2 cm for women. The largest hands on a living person measure 28.5 cm from the wrist to the tip of the middle finger. They belong to Sultan Kösen from Turkey. His hand was measured on 8 February 2011 and the size gained him a Guinness World Record for the largest hands!

Largest hands YR 5

 ## ON YOUR MARKS

a. What is the most common way that bacteria are spread?
b. Why should you rub in between all your fingers when you wash your hands?
c. Why should you wash your hands after handling an animal?
d. How do you think Sultan Kösen feels about having the largest hands? Why?

 ## GET SET

a. How long should it take to wash your hands?
b. What might happen to a cut or graze if you didn't wash your hands before touching it?
c. Why is drying your hands using a hand-drier machine more hygienic than using a towel?
d. Why do you think it is important to dry your hands thoroughly after washing them?

 ## GO FOR GOLD!

a. How long are Sultan Kösen's hands?
b. How does washing your hands help stop the spread of bacteria?
c. What is the main purpose of the poster?
d. How is this poster the same as and different from other posters you have read?

 ## BEYOND THE RECORD

Use a computer to create a poster that encourages children in your school to wash their hands thoroughly. Search the internet for some key facts about hand washing and choose which facts to use on your poster.

25

RECORD-BREAKING COMPREHENSION

FASTEST TALKER

www.kidscorner123.com/learn/language-facts

Kids' corner — Learn and have fun!

What's on | Watch | Learn | Games | Contact

A B C D E F G H I J K **L** M N O P Q R S T U V W X Y Z

Language facts

Did you know there are over 7,000 different languages spoken in the world today? The oldest of these languages are Sanskrit, Sumerian, Hebrew and Basque.

When you hear people talking in foreign languages, what they are saying can often sound very fast, with words blending into each other.

A study carried out in France showed that the fastest spoken language is Japanese, with an average of 7.84 syllables spoken each second!

The fastest talker in the English language is Sean Shannon from Canada. He recited Hamlet's 260-word soliloquy 'To be or not to be' in 23.8 seconds in Edinburgh on 30 August 1995. That's approximately 15 syllables per second. This soliloquy is always used to measure speed talking for this particular Guinness World Record.

Want to be a Guinness World Record holder? Click **here** for Hamlet's 'To be or not to be' soliloquy and see how quickly you can read it!

TALKING TRIVIA

- The term 'fast talker' can be used to describe someone who misleads or tricks people.
- A person who will not stop talking is known as a blatteroon.

Fastest talker YR 5

ON YOUR MARKS

a. How many different languages are spoken in the world today?
b. Why are bullet points used in the 'Talking trivia' section?
c. What does 'blending' mean?
d. Apart from talking, in what other ways can people communicate with each other?

GET SET

a. Name two of the oldest languages in the world.
b. What does the verb 'recited' mean?
c. Why does the author start the main text with a question?
d. What piece of text would *you* use to help measure the fastest talker? Why?

GO FOR GOLD!

a. What is the fastest spoken language in the world?
b. What is a soliloquy?
c. How do you think a fast talker could trick or mislead people?
d. Why do you think the same soliloquy is always used for this record attempt?

BEYOND THE RECORD

How fast can you read out loud? Time yourself reading the first three lines of Hamlet's 'To be or not to be' soliloquy. Count the syllables in the text and work out how many syllables you read per second. Ask a partner to read the same text. Time them and see who is the fastest reader.

27

RECORD-BREAKING COMPREHENSION
TALLEST TEENAGER LIVING (MALE)

Growth

Your height is dependent on several different factors, including the height of your parents, your diet and your general health. In the world today, the average height for an adult male is 175 cm. For an adult female, it is 163 cm.

Rates of growth

During the first year of life, healthy babies can grow a remarkable 25 cm.

From the age of one, a child's rate of growth slows down to around 6 cm per year. However, not all children grow at the same rate. Sometimes growth is slower and sometimes a child has a growth spurt. Interestingly, scientists have shown that children grow slightly faster during spring, compared to other times of the year.

When children reach adolescence (around 8–13 years for girls and 10–15 years for boys), a major growth spurt occurs. This growth spurt usually ends during the middle of the teenage years (between 15–17 years), at which point most individuals will have reached their final 'adult' height.

Height throughout history

The average height of both men and women has changed throughout history. Over time, populations have become taller, mainly because of better nutrition and access to health care.

The picture on the left is of Robert Wadlow (1918–1940), the tallest man ever, who reached a height of 272 cm. In this photograph, he is standing next to his father.

The picture on the right is of Brenden Adams, standing next to his mother. He is the tallest male under the age of 18, measuring 225.1 cm. Brenden suffers from an extremely rare disorder (he is currently the only known case), which has led to his extraordinary height.

Encyclopedia of the Human Body   **47**

Tallest teenager living (male)   YR 5

ON YOUR MARKS

a. What is the average height for an adult male?
b. What is a 'growth spurt'?
c. Why do you think a baby's growth rate slows down after the first year?
d. How do you think Brenden Adams feels about being so tall? Give reasons for your answer.

GET SET

a. At which time of year do children grow slightly faster?
b. What do you notice about the sub-heading 'Height throughout history'? Why has the writer chosen to do this?
c. Why has the author used the adjective 'healthy' when describing the rate at which babies grow?
d. Do you think Robert Wadlow was treated differently because he was the tallest man? Why?

GO FOR GOLD!

a. What happens during adolescence?
b. Why might your diet affect how tall you grow?
c. Why does the author use the adjective 'remarkable' to describe a baby's growth rate?
d. What do you think is the most interesting piece of information in the text? Why?

BEYOND THE RECORD

Use the information in the text to create an interesting PowerPoint® presentation about human growth. Share your presentation with your class and gather feedback. What could you do better next time?

RECORD-BREAKING COMPREHENSION

LARGEST VERTICAL GARDEN (GREEN WALL)

VERTICAL GARDENS

A vertical garden is a wall – or any other vertical surface – that is covered by plants. A vertical garden can also be called a 'green wall'.

A green wall is a great way to increase the area available to grow plants and can be especially useful for people who have small gardens.

The simplest green wall can be created by planting climbing plants at the bottom of a wall. The most complex green walls are created by attaching special modules to a wall and filling them with soil. These are more commonly found on modern hotel and office buildings rather than at private homes. They are beneficial for wildlife and look very attractive.

Green walls can be seen in many cities around the world, such as London, Paris and Madrid.

HOW TO...

Gardening doesn't have to be flat! Try creating your own simple green wall using the steps below:

- Make a frame out of wood.
- Fix metal 'vine eyes' at regular spaces along the frame, about a metre apart.
- Thread strong wire through the vine eyes. Tighten the wires.
- Choose your plants. Plants that are natural climbers work best.
- Plant the climbers in soil or compost, close to the base of the wall.
- As the plants grow, tie them to the framework or wire.

On 23 November 2011, the Hotel Mercure Santo Domingo, in Madrid, Spain, broke the Guinness World Record for the largest vertical garden, measuring an area of 844.05 m^2.

28 HOW TO GARDEN

Largest vertical garden (green wall) YR 5

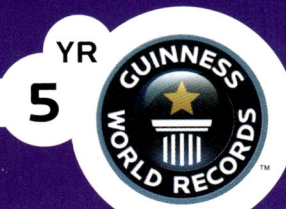

 **ON YOUR MARKS**

a. Why are green walls useful for people with small gardens?
b. What kind of text is provided in the box at bottom left?
c. How might a green wall benefit passers-by?
d. Where would you go to choose plants for a green wall?

 **GET SET**

a. What is the simplest form of green wall?
b. Why would you need to use plants that are 'natural climbers' to create a simple green wall?
c. Why should the modules in complex green walls be filled with soil?
d. Do you think green walls are a good idea? Why?

 **GO FOR GOLD!**

a. How do you make the most complex form of green wall?
b. Why should you tie plants to the frame or wire?
c. How might green walls benefit wildlife?
d. Why do you think complex green walls are found on modern buildings and not private homes?

 **BEYOND THE RECORD**

Think of a place in your local area that could be made more attractive by planting a green wall. Write a persuasive letter to your local council, explaining why it should fund a green-wall project.

31

RECORD-BREAKING COMPREHENSION

LARGEST HAIRY FAMILY

Unusual acts

THE GOMEZ BROTHERS

Congenital Generalised Hypertrichosis is a rare medical condition that leads to excessive hair on the face and body. It is also known as 'Werewolf Syndrome'. In legends, a werewolf is a human who transforms into a wolf-like form.

Danny and Larry Gomez are two brothers from Mexico who have 'Werewolf Syndrome'. They possess thick hair covering 98% of their bodies (only their hands and feet aren't covered). Acting as 'The Wolf People', they perform in the Mexican National Circus as skilled trapeze artists, jugglers and clowns. Their full names are Gabriel Ramos Gomez and Victor Gomez. The duo started performing when they were just six years old.

Together with cousins Louisa Lilia De Lira Aceves and Jesus Manuel Fajardo Aceves, the brothers come from a family of 19. They all have the same inherited condition, which spans five generations. They hold the Guinness World Record for largest hairy family.

Victor Gomez (pictured here) and his brother are covered with thick hair.

14 *Circus Skills*

Largest hairy family YR 5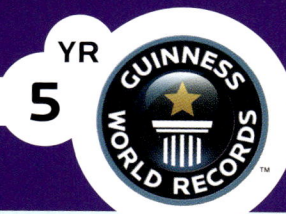

 ## ON YOUR MARKS

a. How old were Danny and Larry when they started performing?
b. Why is Congenital Generalised Hypertrichosis known as 'Werewolf Syndrome'?
c. Why do Danny and Larry Gomez call themselves 'The Wolf People'?
d. Why do you think Danny and Larry chose to become performers?

 ## GET SET

a. Where do Danny and Larry Gomez perform?
b. What does the author mean by 'spans five generations'?
c. Why do you think Gabriel Ramos Gomez and Victor Gomez use the names Danny and Larry?
d. Do you think werewolves are real or imaginary? Why?

 ## GO FOR GOLD!

a. Write down the hyphenated term used in the text.
b. Why do members of the same family suffer from Congenital Generalised Hypertrichosis?
c. Explain the meaning of the adjective 'excessive'.
d. How do you think Danny and Larry feel about being covered with so much hair? Why?

 ## BEYOND THE RECORD

Imagine Danny and Larry are coming to visit your school. Write down a list of five questions you would like to ask them. With a partner, use your questions to role-play an interview with either Danny or Larry. When you have finished, swap roles and repeat the activity.

33

RECORD-BREAKING COMPREHENSION

HEAVIEST VEHICLE PULLED BY HAIR (FEMALE)

How strong is a human hair?

Want to know how strong *your* hair is? Then have a go at our hair-raising experiment!

You will need:
- a strand of hair
- a pencil
- sticky tape
- a pile of books
- several pennies.

What to do

1. Take a strand of your hair. Hold it near the root and pull it out *gently*.
2. Tape the strand of hair to a pencil.
3. Place a pile of books on top of the pencil to anchor it securely. The hair should hang downwards from the pencil.
4. Carefully tape one penny to the end of the hair.
5. Add more pennies, one by one.
6. When the hair breaks, count the number of pennies taped to the hair.
7. To work out the weight your hair can hold, multiply the number of pennies counted by 2.5 g.

Did you know …?

- A whole head of human hair is strong enough to support the weight of two elephants.
- On 3 March 2011, Rani Raikwar from India used her head of hair to pull a vehicle weighing 8,835.5 kg! She broke the Guinness World Record on the set of *Ab India Todega* in Lalitpur, Bhopal. She only needed to pull 3,500 kg to break the female record, but she was determined to beat the male record too, and succeeded!

12 *Sundaze for Kids*

Heaviest vehicle pulled by hair (female) YR 5

ON YOUR MARKS

a. Where should you hold a strand of hair to pull it out?
b. Why are bullet points used in the text?
c. Why should you count the number of pennies used when the strand of hair breaks?
d. Why should you anchor the pencil securely?

GET SET

a. What weight was the vehicle pulled by Rani Raikwar?
b. What does the author do at the start of the text to ensure the audience will keep reading?
c. Why did Rani use her whole head of hair?
d. How do you think Rani prepared for her record attempt?

GO FOR GOLD!

a. How much weight can a whole head of human hair support?
b. In the experiment, why should you 'add more pennies one by one'?
c. Why is the word 'gently' in italics?
d. How is this text similar to other texts you have read?

BEYOND THE RECORD

Carry out experiments to find out the strength of other fine materials, such as cotton, cobwebs, plant fibres or grass. Use the numbered steps in the text to help you. Create a chart to show the results of your experiments.

35

RECORD-BREAKING COMPREHENSION

LARGEST GATHERING OF PEOPLE DRESSED AS LEPRECHAUNS

Leprechauns
Leprechauns are fairy creatures from Irish folklore.

Appearance
Leprechauns look like tiny old men. They are smartly dressed in green, with a hat, suit, waistcoat and buckled shoes.

Occupation
Leprechauns are shoemakers.

Characteristics
- Leprechauns keep all their coins in a large jar, which they bury at the foot of a rainbow.
- Humans think leprechauns are mischief-makers. However, any tricks they play are generally harmless.
- Leprechauns are keen musicians and play tin whistles and Irish harps.

The Guinness World Record for the largest gathering of people dressed as leprechauns was achieved by 1,263 participants in an event organised in Bandon Town, in our very own Ireland, on 17 March 2012!

Catching a leprechaun
Leprechauns are secretive creatures and are rarely seen. Some people would like to catch a leprechaun so they could take his pot of gold. If they did, they would most certainly regret it. Folklore says that a leprechaun will offer the person who captures him three wishes, but then confuse him so much that he is left worse off, as the following legend shows.

A poor man was once so desperate that he decided to seek out a leprechaun in a bid to solve his life's worries. After searching for many months, the man finally found and caught a leprechaun and at once made his first wish: to be rich. The leprechaun bowed and smiled and suddenly the man was surrounded by golden coins. For his second wish, the now-rich man asked to live on a tropical island. The leprechaun looked at the man mischievously and nodded. In a flash, the man was transported to a desert island with no one to talk to and nowhere to spend his money. Realising his mistake, he was forced to waste his third wish on asking to come home.

24 *Guide to Ireland*

Largest gathering of people dressed as leprechauns

YR 5

ON YOUR MARKS

a. What colour do leprechauns wear?
b. What does 'mischievously' mean?
c. Is it easy to find a leprechaun? How do you know?
d. Do you think that leprechauns are dangerous creatures? Why?

GET SET

a. Why are leprechauns rarely seen?
b. How does the author feel about the Guinness World Record? How do you know?
c. Why might someone regret trying to catch a leprechaun?
d. What other information would you like to be included in the text?

GO FOR GOLD!

a. Why would someone want to catch a leprechaun?
b. What went wrong with the poor man's three wishes?
c. Leprechauns come from Irish folklore. What else in the text tells you that leprechauns are fictional creatures?
d. How is this text similar to or different from other tourist information you have read?

BEYOND THE RECORD

Research another creature from folklore. Write a character sketch for this creature.

37

RECORD-BREAKING COMPREHENSION

MOST DECKS OF PLAYING CARDS MEMORISED – SINGLE SIGHTING

www.exam_success.co.uk/memorytips

Exam success

Memory tips

Did you know that there are techniques you can use to help improve your memory? Try out some of the tips below.

- **Visualise it**
  Picture what you want to remember in your mind. The more ridiculous the image, the better.

- **Chain it**
  When you need to remember a number of different things, visualise each one and then link them together with an image.

- **Chunk it**
  Group things into chunks. A phone number is easier to remember when it is broken down into smaller chunks. For example, you could 'chunk' 0127364190 to make 01 273 64190. This technique is also useful for remembering spellings and poems.

- **Acrostic it**
  Create a memorable sentence or phrase in which each word starts with the initial letter of what you want to remember. For example, **M**y **V**ery **E**xcellent **M**other **J**ust **S**erved **U**s **N**achos helps us to remember the order of the planets from the Sun: **M**ercury, **V**enus, **E**arth, **M**ars, **J**upiter, **S**aturn, **U**ranus, **N**eptune.

If you practise these techniques, you might find it easier to remember people's names, lists of numbers, and other facts.

Keep practising and you might develop as good a memory as Dave Farrow from Canada. On 2 April 2007, he memorised a random sequence of 59 separate decks of playing cards at CTV Studios, The Daily Planet in Toronto. That's 3,068 cards on a single sighting!

Sidebar:
- Subjects
- Planning
- Dos and don'ts
- Memory tips
- Contact

38

Most decks of playing cards memorised – single sighting

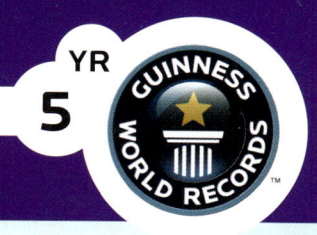

YR 5

ON YOUR MARKS

a. Where does Dave Farrow come from?
b. Why might a ridiculous image help you to remember something?
c. What technique might you use to help you remember the order of a group of things?
d. What does the phrase 'The more ridiculous the image, the better' mean?

GET SET

a. What technique could help you to remember a long number?
b. What advice does the web page give to help you use the memory techniques?
c. Which words and phrases tell you this is a set of instructions?
d. Which memory technique do you think works best? Why?

GO FOR GOLD!

a. What is an acrostic sentence?
b. What is a drawback with using acrostic sentences to remember things?
c. What could go wrong with the order of planets in the acrostic sentence in the web page?
d. What information in the web page shows that having a good memory can be a benefit?

BEYOND THE RECORD

Use the information in the web page to create a three-minute presentation entitled 'Brain training tips'. What key information will you include?

RECORD-BREAKING COMPREHENSION
LARGEST TORCHLIT PARADE

Focus on ... Fire festivals

Playing with fire

Torchlit parades are usually held at night as a celebration of something. People form a procession and parade through the streets, holding torches aloft. The torches are usually made with wax, or from hessian cloth rolled into a tube and then soaked in wax. The burning wax is held by a wooden handle and sometimes a cardboard collar is used to provide protection from any dripping wax.

Many different occasions are marked with a torchlit parade, such as the opening or closing of festivals and sporting events.

A torchlit parade occurs every four years in celebration of the Olympic Games. The torch is lit in Greece and transported to the host country, where it is carried to the opening of the Games by a relay of runners.

A spectacular torchlit parade called Up Helly Aa takes place each year on the Shetland Islands. This Viking Fire Festival has male-only parades of men and boys dressed in Viking and other costumes and carrying flaming torches, which are later thrown into a wooden Viking boat.

In New Orleans, USA, the world-famous Mardi Gras parade features elaborate costumes, floats, and torches called 'flambeaux', which means 'lighted torch' in French.

The record for the largest ever torchlit parade was 3,690 people at the Annual Freedom Celebration 'FFG Love Movement'. It was held on 10 December 2011 at Istora Senayan Stadium in Jakarta, Indonesia and was organised by Freedom Faithnet Global.

48 InFlight

Largest torchlit parade

YR 5

ON YOUR MARKS

a. At what time of day are torchlit parades usually held?
b. Why is the Olympic Torch parade held once every four years?
c. Why do you think people mark the opening or closing of events with torchlit parades?
d. What might happen if a lighted torch had no protection against dripping wax?

GET SET

a. What are the torches made from?
b. Explain the meaning of the word 'aloft'.
c. What do you think happens when flaming torches are thrown into a wooden Viking boat?
d. Which of these torchlit parades is the most famous? Why?

GO FOR GOLD!

a. What does 'flambeaux' mean?
b. Give two reasons why the author might describe the Up Helly Aa parade as 'spectacular'.
c. Why do you think a relay of runners is used to carry the Olympic flame?
d. Do you think women and girls should be allowed to take part in the Up Helly Aa festival? Why?

BEYOND THE RECORD

Imagine you want to be an Olympic torchbearer in the next Olympic Games. Write a persuasive letter to apply to take part in the Torch relay.

RECORD-BREAKING COMPREHENSION

LONGEST FINGERNAILS (FEMALE) – EVER

To: Sonya
Cc:
Subject: Fingernails with a difference!

Hi Sonya,

Hope you are well. Really looking forward to getting together to have our nails painted. I've just been looking at the Guinness World Records website and found out about a record that I thought you'd appreciate.

I was doing some research for a school project and came across a woman called Lee Redmond from Salt Lake City, USA, who broke the Guinness World Record for the longest female fingernails. Lee started growing her nails in 1979.

She has had loads of media attention, including newspaper articles and a feature on CBS News. She had her fingernails officially measured on an Italian TV show called *Lo Show dei Record* on 23 February 2008. They measured 8.65 m in total – can you believe it?

After a bit more research, I found out that Lee still managed to lead a normal life with her record-breaking nails: she could drive a car, hoover the house and even cut her grandchildren's hair. She also managed to care for her husband, who was unwell – what an incredible lady. Apparently, the only thing that she found difficult was putting on a heavy coat – I can understand why!

In 2009, Lee was in a car crash – thankfully she recovered from her injuries, but all her nails were broken off. She still holds the Guinness World Record though. In an interview, she said that it is much easier for her to do things now and her hands seem to 'fly' with the weight of the nails gone.

Check out the photo I've pasted below. Looking forward to seeing you next week!

Bella x

Longest fingernails (female) – ever   YR 5

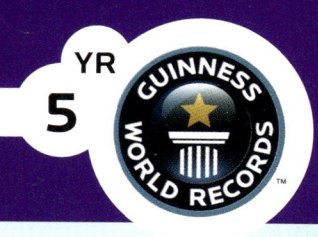

ON YOUR MARKS

a. In what year did Lee Redmond start to grow her nails?
b. Why would putting on a heavy coat be difficult with such long nails?
c. Give one example of informal language used in the text.
d. What else would you like to know about Lee Redmond?

GET SET

a. Where and when were Lee Redmond's nails officially measured?
b. What does 'media attention' mean?
c. Why does Lee Redmond still hold the Guinness World Record even though her nails were broken off?
d. Do you think Lee enjoyed appearing on television? Why?

GO FOR GOLD!

a. Which city does Lee Redmond come from?
b. What did Lee Redmond mean when she said her hands seem to 'fly'?
c. Why might Sonya 'appreciate' this Guinness World Record?
d. Why do you think Bella calls Lee 'an incredible lady'?

BEYOND THE RECORD

What would your day be like with very long fingernails? Write a list of your everyday activities, such as cleaning your teeth and getting dressed. Create a scale and grade each activity on your list from easy to impossible.

RECORD-BREAKING COMPREHENSION

SHORTEST LIVING WOMAN

A SHORT STORY
Jyoti Amge

Everyone is different. Some people are tall, some are short, some are slim and some are muscular. Aspiring to look the same as someone else isn't helpful; what may be an ideal size for one person may be unhealthy for someone else.

The shortest woman in the world, Jyoti Amge from Nagpur, India, shows that regardless of our size or shape, everyone can achieve their goals and live happy and fulfilling lives. Jyoti has a form of dwarfism and measures just 62.8 cm. She refuses to let her size hold her back in life.

Although much smaller than her classmates, Jyoti was never treated differently by her school friends. They accepted her for who she was, not what she looked like.

Jyoti already held the record for the world's smallest teen, but on her 18th birthday, amid a large press presence, she was recognised as the shortest living woman by Guinness World Records. After the announcement, she tearfully told reporters that this was an 'extra birthday present'.

One day Jyoti would like to be an actress in Bollywood. Her ambition doesn't stop there – she is currently pursuing a career in politics.

The name Jyoti means 'the light'. Jyoti is certainly a shining example of how being different should not affect what we can achieve in life.

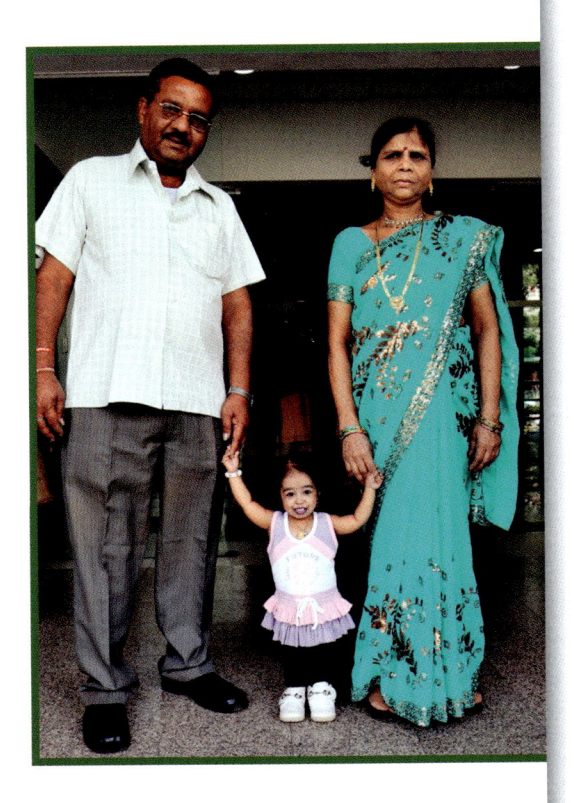

36   Weekender / Saturday 27 October, 2012

Shortest living woman YR 5

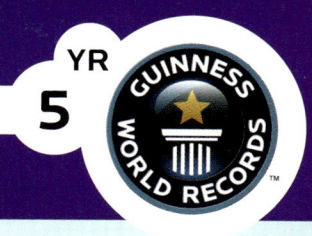

ON YOUR MARKS

a. Who is the shortest woman in the world?
b. What does 'aspiring to look the same as someone else' mean?
c. Why was Jyoti crying on her 18th birthday?
d. Do you admire Jyoti? Why?

GET SET

a. What does Jyoti want to do in Bollywood?
b. What do you think the author is trying to achieve in this text?
c. What does 'press presence' mean?
d. How does the author want you to feel about Jyoti? Provide evidence from the text to support your answer.

GO FOR GOLD!

a. Write down the connective word used in the fourth paragraph.
b. What is the name for this kind of recount?
c. Why has the author used the word 'shining' in the last paragraph?
d. Is Jyoti treated differently because of her size? Explain your answer.

BEYOND THE RECORD

Use three internet sources to find out more about Jyoti Amge. Imagine Jyoti is travelling from India to visit your school. What three questions would you ask her that you cannot answer from your internet research?

RECORD-BREAKING COMPREHENSION

LARGEST DRUMMING LESSON

MUSIC NEWS

London Schools Newsletter
The award-winning newsletter for London's teachers

To become a professional drummer of a five-piece drum kit, you need to learn how to create complicated rhythms using both your hands and feet at the same time. Plenty of practice is required and a good teacher makes all the difference!

But you *don't* need to be a professional to create simple rhythms in your class. All you need is a surface to beat, either with your hands or with a stick.

On 25 May, 242 primary schoolchildren and 18 teachers from Greater London took part in the largest ever drumming session at Chessington World of Adventures in Surrey, UK. The event was organised to mark Africa Day, which celebrates African diversity and success.

The participants used traditional African drums, made of a hollowed-out wooden 'shell' covered by animal skin. They were initially taught how to warm up and then shown different drumming techniques and the principles of rhythm. The 30-minute lesson ended with the performance of a drumming sequence, which the whole group had learned.

The atmosphere created by 260 people all drumming the same rhythm at the same time was a unique experience for children and staff alike!

4 June 2011

Largest drumming lesson YR 5

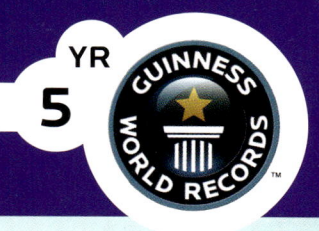

ON YOUR MARKS

a. Where did the largest drumming lesson take place?
b. Why don't you need to be a professional drummer to play a simple rhythm?
c. Why would having a good teacher make 'all the difference'?
d. Why do you think this particular event was organised to mark Africa Day?

GET SET

a. How long did the largest drumming lesson last?
b. Do you think the author wants to encourage or discourage events like these? Why?
c. What does 'drumming techniques' mean?
d. Do you think you would have enjoyed taking part in this record attempt? Why?

GO FOR GOLD!

a. Write down the word in the text that means 'variety'.
b. Give two reasons why the children and teachers played traditional African drums.
c. How important was it for everyone to drum the same rhythm at the end of the lesson? Why?
d. Would you prefer to play an African drum or a five-piece drum kit? Explain your answer.

BEYOND THE RECORD

Use three different sources to find out more about different kinds of traditional drums from around the world, including where they are from and how they are played. Create an information sheet for three of these drums.

RECORD-BREAKING COMPREHENSION
DEEPEST SCUBA DIVE IN SEA WATER

News

SOUTH AFRICAN BREAKS SCUBA-DIVE RECORD

On 10 June 2005, Nuno Gomes from South Africa broke the Guinness World Record for the deepest scuba dive in sea water. He dived to an incredible depth of 318.25 m in the Red Sea off Dahab, Egypt.

Going down ...

Early in the morning, Nuno's team went aboard the *NABQ Explorer* in Dahab and left for the diving point, 4 km off shore.

Once there, the team dropped a long line linked to a weight onto the seabed to help Nuno dive more safely. Then they dropped over a weight that had special labels on it. He had to bring these back as proof that he had broken the record.

Forty minutes after Nuno had dived into the Red Sea, another diver dived down to 124 m – to check on his progress, and to see if he was safe and well. When the diver came back up, he tied two message labels onto a marker buoy for Nuno's team to pick up. The messages were: 'OK' and 'World Record'.

Coming back up ...

However, the dive was not over. Nuno had dived so far down, his body needed more oxygen. It was important that he didn't come back up too quickly, or he could die.

Rising quickly through the water is dangerous. A quick change in air pressure can make a diver ill. This is called 'decompression', or 'the bends'.

So, at points along the line, Nuno rested and took more oxygen. Eleven hours and 35 minutes later, Nuno finally came back up – as a Guinness World Record holder.

Buoy: a weighted float that marks points in the water.

In the photo above, Nuno was around 10 hours into his dive. He was very tired. He is in the middle of the picture, with one support diver on each side. He is using a decompression bar to help him come back up safely.

Nuno and his team can be seen here celebrating after breaking the Guinness World Record.

Diving Monthly

Deepest scuba dive in sea water YR 5 GUINNESS WORLD RECORDS

ON YOUR MARKS

a. How deep did Nuno dive?
b. How do you think Nuno felt when he had finished the record-breaking dive?
c. Why did he need a team to help him?
d. Who do you think might read this article? Why?

GET SET

a. Where did Nuno set his world record?
b. What is the *NABQ Explorer*?
c. What do you think the message label 'OK' meant?
d. Would you like to dive to great depths, like Nuno? Why?

GO FOR GOLD!

a. Why did Nuno have to bring back special labels?
b. Why did the long weighted line help Nuno?
c. What is the main danger that Nuno faced during his record-breaking dive?
d. What do you think is the most interesting piece of information in this article? Why?

BEYOND THE RECORD

Write five questions you would like to ask Nuno. In pairs, take it in turns to be Nuno and the person asking him questions. When you are playing the role of interviewer, make a note of the answers that 'Nuno' gives.

RECORD-BREAKING COMPREHENSION
STRANGEST DIET

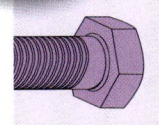

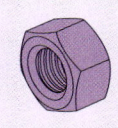

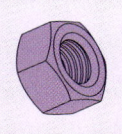

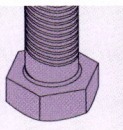

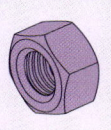

Entertainers

INCREDIBLE EATING

Do you want chips with that?
Michel Lotito was a French entertainer known as Monsieur Mangetout (Mr Eat Everything) who was famous for eating things that would kill the average human being. He holds the Guinness World Record for the strangest diet.

Lotito was born in Grenoble on 15 June 1950 and discovered his rare skill in 1959 when he began trying out the taste of metal. He became an entertainer, eating strange and bizarre 'foods' for the amusement of the public. On average, he consumed 900 g of metal a day.

DO NOT TRY THIS AT HOME!
Michel Lotito's ability to consume metal would kill other human beings.

Strangest diet
From 1966, Lotito consumed 18 bicycles, 15 shopping trolleys, 7 televisions, 6 chandeliers, 2 beds, 1 pair of skis, 1 Cessna light aircraft (this 'meal' took him two years), 1 computer, a small piece of the Eiffel Tower and a 400-m steel chain. He even ate a coffin; the only ever example of a coffin ending up inside a man instead of the other way round!

To ease the passage of this 'food' through his intestines, he broke the items into small pieces and drank oil and water during each 'meal'. The only real foods to upset his stomach were bananas and boiled eggs.

Michel Lotito died on 25 June 2007 of natural causes, aged 57.

Strangest diet YR 5

ON YOUR MARKS

a. Where was Michel Lotito born?
b. What does the phrase 'natural causes' mean?
c. Why is Michel Lotito's skill described as 'rare'?
d. Do you think eating metal was painful for Michel Lotito?

GET SET

a. On average, how much metal did Michel Lotito consume each day?
b. How do you think drinking oil and water helped him to eat the metal?
c. In what way could eating metal be harmful?
d. Why are the words 'food' and 'meal' given inside quotation marks?

GO FOR GOLD!

a. How many shopping trolleys did Michel Lotito consume?
b. Why do you think it took two years to eat the Cessna?
c. What effect do you think the author wants the sub-heading 'Do you want chips with that?' to have on readers?
d. Why did the author include the 'coffin inside a man' comment?

BEYOND THE RECORD

Write 100 words summarising the life achievements of someone from history.

RECORD-BREAKING COMPREHENSION
LARGEST GYMNASTIC DISPLAY (FEMALE)

Unusual destinations

Eastern promise

Want to experience a holiday like no other? Then try the Democratic People's Republic of Korea (DPRK).

This mysterious country is one of the last few remaining Communist countries in the world. The capital, Pyongyang, is the most visited destination in the DPRK. Most tourists to the DPRK come from Communist China, but more and more tourists from the UK visit each year.

There are many sites to see in Pyongyang.

The Arch of Triumph
The arch was designed to commemorate Korean resistance to Japan between 1925 and 1945 and liberation from Japanese rule. Modelled on the Arc de Triomphe in Paris, France, it is the biggest victory arch in the world.

The Juche Tower
This 170 m tall monument offers great views of the city.

Arirang Mass Games
This is a must-see event. It is held in the gigantic May Day Stadium, which holds 150,000 spectators.

Important information

- You will need a visa to enter the DPRK. This can be a lengthy and complicated process so you should apply well in advance of your trip.

- Local guides will accompany you when you visit any of the tourist sites. Unaccompanied trips are strongly discouraged and frowned upon by the authorities.

The stadium itself holds the Guinness World Record for the largest gymnastic display, after 100,090 people took part on 14 August 2007. The organisers of the display were the Grand Mass Gymnastic and Artistic Performance 'Arirang' State Preparing Committee.

InFlight 45

Largest gymnastic display (female) — YR 5 — GUINNESS WORLD RECORDS

ON YOUR MARKS

a. What is the capital city of the DPRK?
b. What is the advantage of applying for a visa well in advance of your trip?
c. Why do you think most visiting tourists come from China?
d. What does the author mean by 'must-see event'?

GET SET

a. Where is the Arirang Mass Games held?
b. What does the verb 'commemorate' mean?
c. Why does the guide say that the DPRK is a holiday destination 'like no other'?
d. Does this information make you want to visit Pyongyang? Why?

GO FOR GOLD!

a. How many spectators does the May Day Stadium hold?
b. In the first main paragraph of text, two countries are abbreviated. What is the reason for doing this?
c. What could the author have abbreviated in the last paragraph?
d. Why do you think the DPRK is described as 'mysterious'?

BEYOND THE RECORD

Use the internet to research unusual holiday destinations. What destination would you most like to visit? Describe the destination, say why it is unusual and why you would like to visit.

RECORD-BREAKING COMPREHENSION

LARGEST ATLAS

www.encyclopedia-file.com/largest-atlas

Maps

Since the Iron Age, people have created and used maps as tools to help them understand, explain and find their way around the world.

A cartographer is a person who creates maps. A collection of maps in the form of a book is called an atlas.

The first person to use the term 'atlas' was Gerardus Mercator (1512–1594). He created a map of the world to help navigators find their way around the Earth. It was the first map that interpreted the globe in a flat, two-dimensional form.

Largest atlas

The largest atlas in the world is Earth Platinum, published by Millennium House (Australia). The atlas measures 1.854 m high, 1.45 m wide and is 6 cm thick. It was measured at the British Library in London, UK, on 13 July 2012.

The atlas is estimated to weigh 200 kg and consists of 61 pages of maps. Only 31 copies of the atlas were printed and each copy costs £64,000. Over 100 professionals from around the globe helped to create the atlas, including 24 photographers and 88 cartographers.

Each map in Earth Platinum was produced using satellite images and a photographic technique that overlays thousands of photographs to create a single, seamless image.

Largest atlas — YR 5 — Guinness World Records

ON YOUR MARKS

a. What is an atlas?
b. What hyphenated term is used in the text to mean 'flat'?
c. How is an atlas different from a globe?
d. Why do you think only 31 copies of Earth Platinum were printed?

GET SET

a. What does a cartographer do?
b. Why is Earth Platinum so expensive? Give two reasons.
c. What do modern cartographers have to help them create maps, which Mercator did not have?
d. Why do you think people wanted to 'find their way around the Earth' in the 1500s?

GO FOR GOLD!

a. When did people start to create maps?
b. What does the word 'seamless' mean?
c. Why might satellite images be used to create a map?
d. Why might someone visit this web page?

BEYOND THE RECORD

Create a map to help visitors find their way around your school. Use a key to explain the different features of your map.

55

READING SKILLS

There are different skills you need to learn when reading texts.

Each AF (assessment focus) describes a different set of reading skills. In this book, you will actively practise and improve your ability to do the following.

AF2:

- Find information in a text.
- Find evidence in a text.

AF3:

- Understand what the writer means but does not tell you directly.

AF4:

- Find patterns in a text.
- Comment on organisation of texts.

AF5:

- Understand why the writer chooses a word.
- Understand why writers sometimes use very short sentences.
- Comment on how a writer uses language for effect.

AF6:

- Identify the writer's purpose.
- Understand the writer's viewpoint and the overall effect of the text.

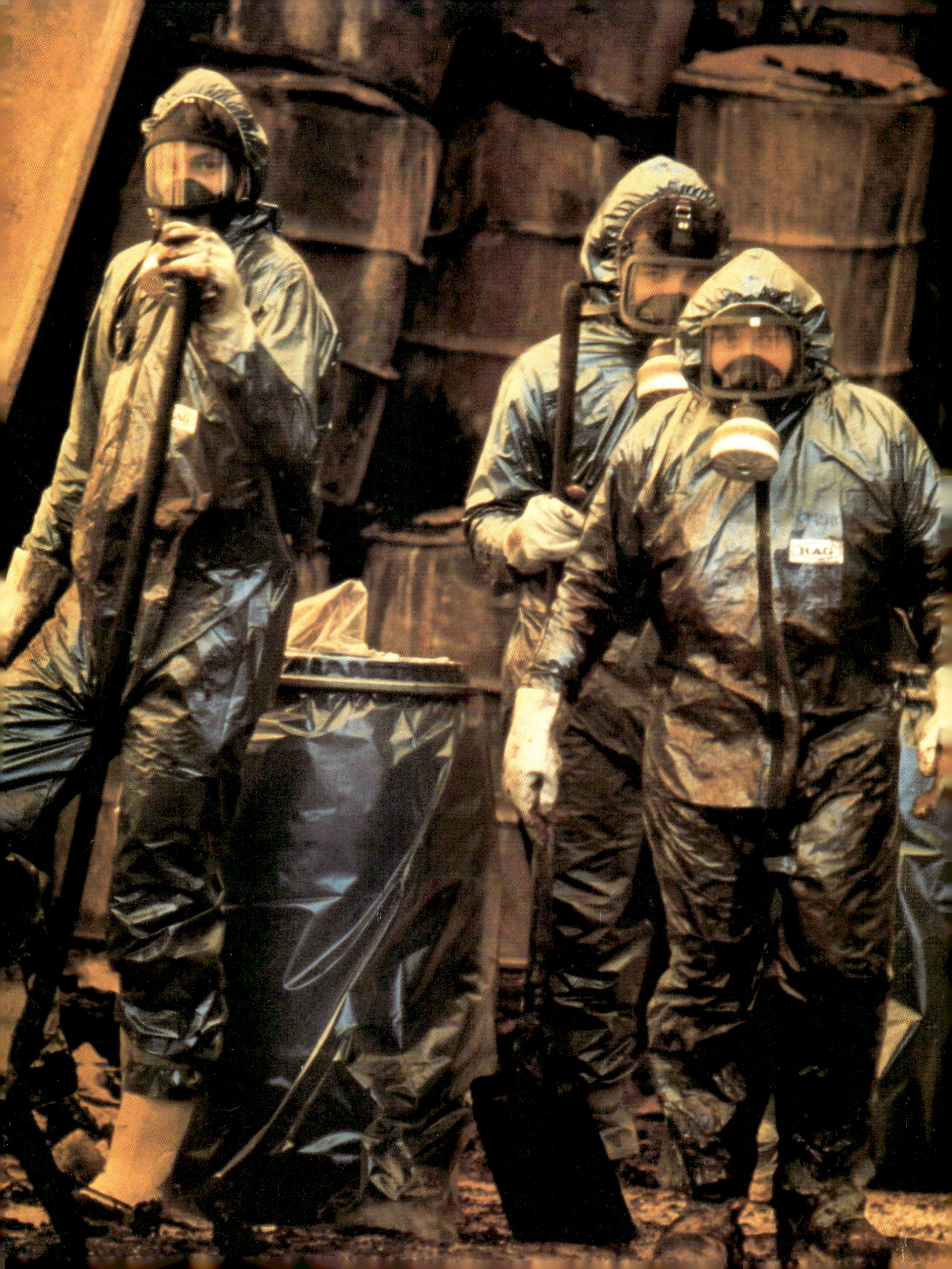
RAG

THE ENVIRONMENT

Adam Markham

Wayland

World Issues

A Divided World
Endangered Wildlife
Food or Famine?
Human Rights
International Terrorism
Nuclear Weapons
Population Growth
Refugees
The Arms Trade
The Energy Crisis
The Environment
The International Debt Crisis
The International Drugs Trade
World Health

Cover: Deforestation in Panama
Frontispiece: Men in protective clothing at the scene of the Sandoz warehouse fire (November 1986)

Editors: Clare Pumfrey/Jannet King
Series Designer: David Armitage

First published in 1988 by
Wayland (Publishers) Ltd,
61 Western Road, Hove
East Sussex, BN3 1JD, England

© Copyright 1988 Wayland (Publishers) Ltd

British Library Cataloguing in Publication Data
Markham, Adam
  The environment. – (World issues).
  1. Human ecology
  I. Title   II. Series
  333.7   GF141

  ISBN 1-85210-141-5

Phototypeset by Kalligraphics Ltd, Redhill, Surrey
Printed and bound in Italy by Sagdos S.p.A., Milan

Contents

1. This fragile planet   6
2. Shaping our environment   9
3. Air pollution   15
4. The changing wilderness   21
5. Seas at risk   30
6. Working for the environment   36
7. What can I do?   41
Glossary   44
Books to read   45
Further information   46
Index   47

1 This fragile planet

What is the environment? It is not only the rolling English countryside or the wild virgin forest of New Guinea, although they are both different types of environment. Our environment is where we are at any time. It includes all our surroundings, both natural and man-made. You can call the house you live in your environment, or the town, or even the country. Every influence on you is part of your environment, from the air you breathe to the water you bathe in.

You, in turn, influence your environment in many different ways. When you light a bonfire, switch on the radio, or throw away a chocolate wrapper, you are affecting your surroundings.

We are all part of the much wider environment of the whole world. Our own actions will have an effect on this wider environment as well. Imagine, for example, a trip to a grocer's shop. Someone, at some time, decided where to build the shop, chose the design of the building and built the road leading to it. By doing this, they changed the environment. The fruits and vegetables inside the shop come from all over the world and have been grown using various farming methods. They may be avocado pears from an Israeli kibbutz, sugar from the plantations of Fiji, and grapes from Argentina. Each farmer involved in the production of these foods has had an effect on the environment. In tropical countries, for example, where pineapples are grown, large areas of rain forest have been cut down to make room for much more intensive farming for export. So, when you buy a pineapple you are indirectly contributing to the damage to the environment in that distant country. Producing energy affects the environment and transporting all these foods from where they were grown to your local shop will have used large amounts of it.

As you drive home with your shopping, the

Forest has been cleared to create space to grow these grapes in Argentina.

exhaust fumes from your car contribute to the pollution of the air. Hundreds of different chemicals, mostly gases, pour out of exhaust pipes. The fumes are harmful to humans, animals and plants. The refrigerator in which you store the food runs on electricity, and choices will have been made about the electricity supply. It could come from a nuclear power station or from a power station fired by oil or coal. If you lived in Norway, it might have been generated by wave power. Links can be made between almost every human activity and the environment. These are just a few of the ways in which we have a direct or indirect influence.

The study of the different relationships between living organisms and their environment

The earth from space, showing the polar ice-cap and northern hemisphere. It is easy to see how the effects of pollution can travel round the globe.

is called ecology. Ecology enables us to build up a picture of the complex web of relationships between organisms and their surroundings, which are called an ecosystem. It includes the relationships between different living organisms and also the non-living influences on them, such as climate and the availability of food and shelter. If we are able to build up a detailed picture of an ecosystem, then we are able to predict how various changes in the environment will affect certain animals and plants.

An environmental crisis

Ecosystems are fragile. When people talk about the 'environmental crisis' they mean that humans are altering the environment in such a way that the delicate balance of various ecosystems, indeed of the global ecosystem, is being destroyed. The felling of tropical rain forests, for example, continues despite the warnings given by scientists. The interests of timber companies and financially hard-pressed governments in developing countries are thought to

Gold has been discovered in the forests of southern Ecuador. The gold-mining companies clear the forests to build roads and camps and the mine workers shoot the wildlife, disturbing the environment.

be more important than the saving of trees.

Wildlife is being hunted to the point of extinction, although some warnings have been heeded. Many species of whales were allowed to reach the brink of extinction before governments agreed that whaling should stop. The world's seas and rivers continue to be polluted and deserts are being created.

We depend on clean, productive oceans to provide us with fish and other foods. Fertile agricultural land is essential to produce food for the whole human population. Clean air is vital both for our health and because air pollution can have far-reaching and disastrous effects on climate, soil and water resources. The result of the environmental crisis is that, in many parts of the world, humans are beginning to struggle to obtain enough food, fuel and clean water for their survival.

2 Shaping our environment

Since the dawn of civilization humankind has shaped its environment. Primitive cave paintings tell us how ancient peoples related to their surrounding, and over the centuries that followed we know that great civilizations grew up around natural features, such as coastal bays or flood-plains. The ancient Egyptians, Sumerians, Greeks and Inca at different times and in different parts of the world developed their societies in harmony with the environment. Changes in the natural environment brought changes in human distribution. Ephesus, the ruins of which are in what is now Turkey, was once a centre for world trade, a part of Alexander the Great's empire, and the site of one of the Seven Wonders of the World. Its economy and the great wealth of its citizens depended on the city's position at the mouth of the fertile river Maeander; but by the sixth century the harbour, rebuilt once already, had almost completely silted up, and so trade moved to the nearby port of Smyrna.

Carthage in North Africa was a prosperous city driven into decline by largely natural forces. At one time, the Phoenicians ruled the Mediterranean region from Carthage. The fertile plains and hills of what is now Tunisia and Algeria provided them with corn and other crops in abundance, but a combination of overgrazing by herd animals, and changing weather in North Africa turned the region into barren wasteland.

The changing landscape

Since ancient times the world has become a very different place indeed. There has been an explosion in human population and astounding advances in technical and scientific knowledge. In most areas of the world the delicate relationship between humankind and nature has been lost. Nature has long since been overrun. Agricultural revolutions, industrial advances and the consumer appetite of modern people have wrought havoc with the environment. Regions that for millenia could support vegetation are being turned to desert, lakes are becoming sterile and species are becoming extinct at a rate of more than ten a day.

The first step towards halting this alarming and catastrophic environmental decline is to understand how humans are contributing to the changes. The landscape of Britain today is entirely the product of human activities. Once clothed almost entirely in mixed and deciduous forest, the countryside now has one of the lowest ratios of trees to surface area of any land in Europe. Trees have been chopped down to provide timber for fires, boats, building, fences and pit props, or simply to clear land for grazing or arable farming. The hedges of today's Britain have only existed for a few hundred years, most of them, in fact, appeared after the Enclosure Acts were passed in the early nineteenth century, yet we are struggling to preserve those hedges that remain intact. More than half of Britain's hedges have been pulled up since the Second World War to make room for intensive agriculture and giant fields.

Agriculture

Humankind has probably had the biggest influence on the environment throughout history, through agriculture and land-use. Nomadic tribes have driven their herds across grasslands for hundreds of years. Slash and burn cultivators have moved through the forests for a similar period. So, why do we have a problem now? The answer is that with the development of land for intensive agriculture, the building of cities or industrial complexes, the land available for traditional subsistence farming has been drastically reduced. In addition, intensive agriculture demands a large return on investment, and so as crop after crop drains the soil of nutrients, farmers become locked into a cycle where they need to apply more fertilizer every year just to achieve the same yield.

The demands of energy have probably had the second greatest effect on the environment. With the industrial revolution in Europe came the machine age. Suddenly, more fuel was needed to keep the factories running. With the new technology came air and water pollution, mine spoils, the abandonment of the countryside by rural peasants looking for work in the cities and the search for ever more efficient ways of producing energy. That search continues today.

African oil-palm plants in Ecuador in an area once covered by tropical rain forest. It is planned that the plantation will stretch to more than 40,000 hectares by 1995.

Energy production

Since the 1940s most of the electricity in Europe and North America has been supplied by burning fossil fuels like gas, coal and oil in large power stations. A dirty process, but one that produced cheap, plentiful electricity. But fuel supplies will not last for ever and with public concern about the effects of acid rain, the demand for more nuclear power has strengthened. Supposedly cheap and clean, nuclear power is thought by many to be the answer to the world's energy problems. Opponents, however, point to the safety risks involved with radiation and the connection between the nuclear arms race and nuclear power. They say that because dangerous radioactive wastes need to be stored away from humans for thousands of years, there are risks involved which are too great to ignore. After all, who will look after the waste dumps when we are gone?

A video picture of the Chernobyl nuclear power station after the fire which released radiation into the atmosphere.

The greatest fear, however, associated with nuclear power is the potential for a serious accident at a power station. The worst nuclear accident to date happened at Chernobyl in the Ukraine in April 1986. Towns nearby had to be permanently evacuated and crops and livestock throughout Europe and Scandinavia were contaminated and subsequently destroyed. Many people died from acute radiation sickness, and the increased number of cancer sufferers in the worst affected countries will not be known for decades to come.

The increasing demand for energy is partly due to the apparently never-ending demand of the average consumer for new products. This is fuelled by advertising. In addition, products are not designed to last very long – known as 'built-in obsolescence' – so when we throw something away, we have to buy a replacement.

Attempting to wash off the radioactive contamination from lorries during the clean-up operation after the Chernobyl disaster. In fact the radiation will just drain away with the water into the soil and stay there, maybe for thousands of years.

Industrial pollution

As a result of the consumer boom, factories have sprung up anywhere that there is a market. Consequently, industrial pollution is a major problem for many communities. This type of pollution is often a local problem only. Effluent from industrial processes is poured, often untreated, into the sea or a local river, killing fish and insects and endangering human health. The air is polluted by the gases and the toxic metals, like lead and cadmium, pouring out of factory chimneys. But the most frightening and visible threat is that of an accident. One of the worst in recent years was the accident at Bhopal in India in December 1984. A factory belonging to the American conglomerate Union Carbide, which manufactured pesticides, exploded, throwing chemical toxins all over the surrounding town. More than 2,000 people died, and at least 4,000 were seriously injured. Industrial accidents which are less serious happen every hour of every day of every year somewhere in the world.

Manufactured goods have to be transported to the point of sale or use. In the case of pesticides, they are often made in Europe and North America and then exported to the developing world. Some, like DDT, are banned in most Western countries but are still widely exported to countries such as India and the Sahel states of Africa. Commercial traffic has existed between countries since the first trade routes were opened up by the Phoenicians and other early civilizations. Transport over long distances has become commonplace. The building of roads, railways, canals and airports has had its effect on the environment.

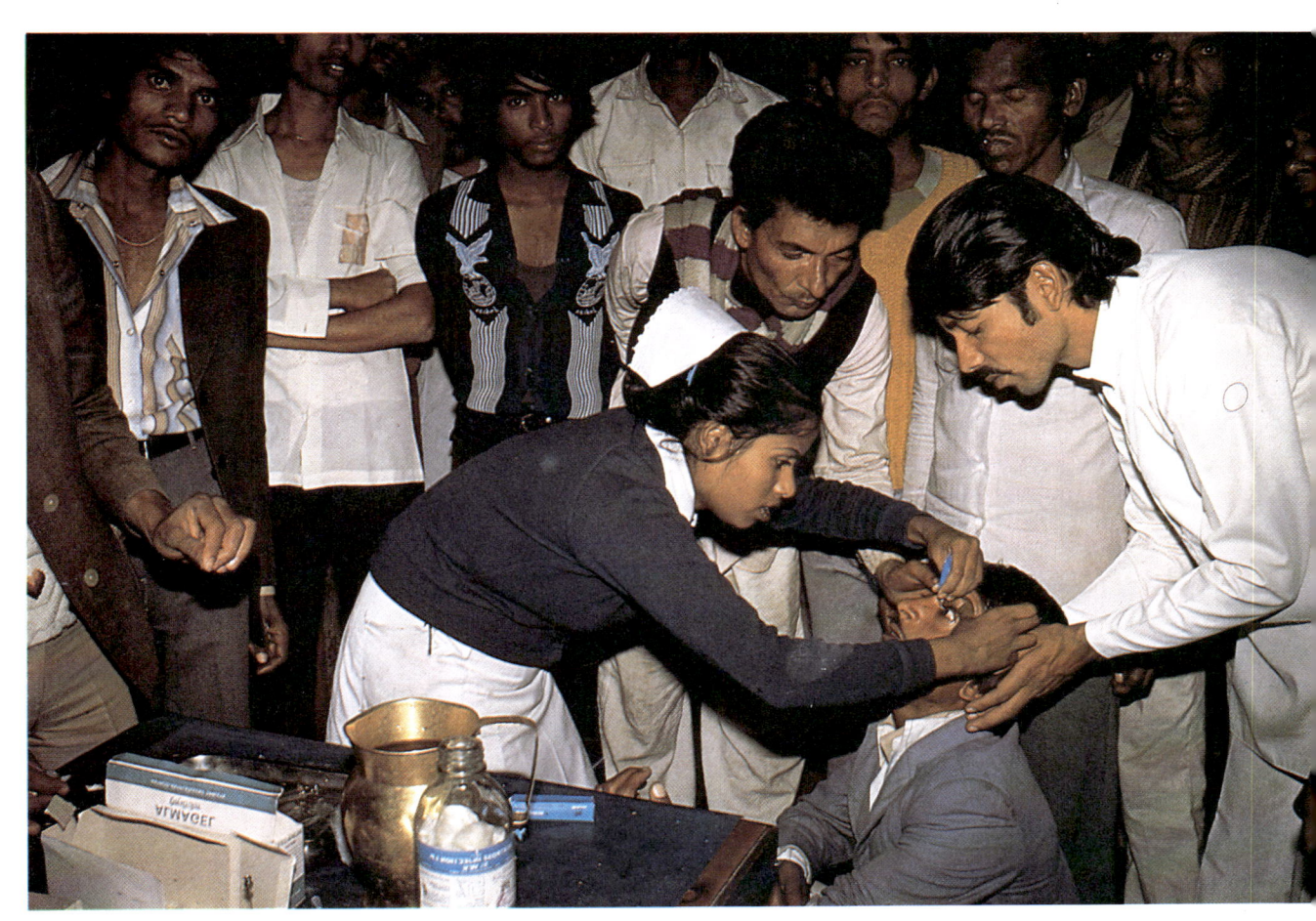

One of the effects of the gases released in the Bhopal accident was damage to the eyes.

Urban development

Much of the distribution of plants in Britain, for example, can be explained by the development of the railways in the early nineteenth century. Similarly, the opening up of tropical rain forests to disturbing influences can often be put down to the driving of roads through virgin forest. It has been shown many times by researchers that building roads attracts cars in greater numbers, increasing congestion and causing accidents, rather than actually easing the flow of traffic. The transport systems which least damage the environment are those that combine public transport, like trams, buses and trains, with a road system. Most important of all is to take into account the needs of pedestrians and cyclists. Cars are the cause of much of the stress of urban living. If town planners had not, in places like Birmingham, concentrated on getting cars through the city centre then the people who live there would no doubt be both healthier and happier. Roads through cities often cut communities in two. Pollution

Millions of Chinese cycle to work every day. Some of them wear face masks to try and stop harmful fumes from entering their lungs.

from the diesel fumes from lorries and the exhaust of cars presents a real hazard for urban dwellers; and cyclists often seem to be completely ignored. Some countries have tried to tackle the problem of urban living very seriously. In the Netherlands all town planning for many years has taken account of the needs of the people living there rather than the cars passing through. Facilities for cyclists are the best in the world, and consequently more people per head of population than anywhere else go to work by bike.

The planners of the future, whether involved in agriculture, industry, the energy sector or inner city development will have to take into account the needs not just of a changing and sensitive environment, but of the people who share it. If we care for our environment and don't waste our resources, ultimately we are caring for ourselves as well.

3
Air pollution

It is difficult to single out one environmental issue for special attention. Air pollution, however, is of particular significance on a global scale. A healthy environment depends above everything on clean air and this is a legacy that most people would wish to leave to future generations. Avoiding the catastrophic results of acid rain, the warming of the environment (or 'greenhouse effect') and the breakdown of the stratospheric ozone layer, is a huge challenge to human inventiveness.

These three related problems are discussed more and more frequently by environmentalists, politicians and scientists. A hundred years ago, most people would never have heard of acid rain, but few would have been in any doubt as to what air pollution was. In the past, air pollution was seen as a local problem, affecting only those who lived near factories that belched out smoke and fumes, or in cities where the smoke from thousands of domestic hearths clouded the air. However, poisonous gases, such as sulphur dioxide and nitrogen oxides, are able to travel hundreds, even thousands, of kilometres in the air before falling to the ground as acids and thus affecting areas remote from industry. Over the last forty years air pollution has been recognized as an international problem.

As with many environmental problems, it was not until humankind itself was endangered that a threat was recognized at all. Despite years of increasing air pollution throughout the industrialized countries, alarm bells only started to ring when a terrible smog engulfed London in the 1940s and 1950s. For a week in December of 1952 a cloud of smoke mixed with fog hung over the city. It blocked sunlight from the streets and is thought to have been responsible for the deaths of over 4,000 people. This toll on human life led to the introduction of the world's first major air pollution law – the Clean Air Act of 1956. The effect of this piece of legislation has been to clear the air in London. Since then, the situation has improved enormously.

A London street in the smog in 1948. Although it looks like night-time, the picture was actually taken during the day.

Acid rain

The Clean Air Act was followed by similar laws in many other countries. The main aim was to cut down on smoke pollution. Unfortunately, however, these laws did little to clean up the invisible gases that were emitted from power stations, particularly sulphur dioxide and the various oxides of nitrogen. It is these invisible gases which are largely responsible for acid rain today.

'Acid rain' is now widely used to describe not just acidic deposits, but the whole complex chemical cocktail which pollutes our atmosphere. Although the term acid rain was coined after studies of precipitation in Manchester in 1872, the first significant scientific work on the problem really began in Scandinavia in the 1960s. It was prompted by reports from fishermen of declining catches from year to year, and mass deaths of trout and salmon at snowmelt time. Scientific detective work revealed that it was acid accumulating in the snow and water that was causing the damage to fish stocks. In addition, acid rain was causing toxic metals such as aluminium and mercury to be released from the soil and washed out, or leached, into the rivers and lakes. Aluminium is particularly harmful to fish, building up a white scum on their gills that prevents efficient breathing and interferes with the exchange of blood salts and oxygen. Today, more than 13,000 sq km of lakes and rivers in southern Norway are dead or dying, and the seven most important salmon rivers in Norway have lost nearly all their fish. Other countries are suffering too. Thousands of lakes in Canada are affected and West Germany, Holland, Britain and Poland are just some of the countries where lakes have become devoid of life.

In the Black Forest in southern Germany nearly three-quarters of the trees are dead or dying as a result of acid rain.

Water acidification is not the only result of acid rain. Soil scientists in West Germany started saying in 1981 that acidification of the soil in some parts of the country had reached such a serious level that trees would no longer be able to live. Sure enough, by the time of the national West German Forest Survey in 1983, 30 per cent of the country's trees were found to be damaged. The devastation was not confined to small areas or to single species (although some, such as the silver fir, appeared to be especially sensitive), but affected the whole of the nation's forest stock. By November 1986, 54 per cent of West Germany's trees were damaged, with millions of trees already dead.

This phenomenon was called *Waldsterben*, or forest death, and world scientific opinion blames it on a mixture of air pollutants. *Waldsterben* is spreading through the industrialized countries. In Switzerland, more than half of the forest is damaged and some villages have had to be evacuated because of the increased danger of avalanches when the trees that stabilize the soil on steep slopes die. In Canada, the maple syrup industry is threatened by *Waldsterben* and in the USA tree death is reaching epidemic proportions in Vermont and in the Adirondack mountains.

Much of the stonework of Westminster Abbey in London has had to be replaced because the original stonework was so badly damaged by air pollution.

The exact combination of air pollutants that kills the trees is not known. The concentrations of individual chemicals differ from area to area. The composition of local soils is important, with the worst damage occurring where the soils are least able to neutralize acids. However, the most lethal combination of air pollutants for trees seems to be acid mists and ozone combined. Ozone is another of the invisible pollutants, formed largely as a result of chemical reactions between some of the exhaust gases of cars. Ozone is important when it is high above the earth, forming a layer of the stratosphere and protecting us from the sun's harmful ultraviolet radiation, but at ground level it is a serious pollutant that can damage human health as well as trees and crops.

Cleaning up

Apart from the deaths of lakes and trees, acid rain causes damage to agriculture, buildings (including such famous examples as the Acropolis and St Paul's Cathedral), wildlife, human health and even the marine ecosystem. The costs of this damage are huge. To reduce these damaging effects, we must begin by identifying the main sources and then develop the technology to decrease their output. The main sources of air pollutants are power stations which burn fossil fuels, and motor cars. The technology already exists to clean up both of these sources substantially.

Power stations produce most of the sulphur dioxide that contributes to acid rain, and some of the nitrogen oxides. Motor cars produce most of the nitrogen oxides and other pollutants, such as lead (in countries like Britain, where lead-free petrol is not compulsory), carbon monoxide and hydrocarbons. The hydrocarbons combine with the nitrogen oxides in sunlight to form ozone. Another major source of sulphur pollution is metal smelters. These are particularly significant in the USA and Eastern Europe.

Scientists from the Nordic Council and from the United Nations working groups on acid rain have suggested that if we are to protect the most sensitive habitats from damage then we need to set limits for nitrogen and sulphur depositions worldwide. These limits are likely to require reductions in emissions of 80–90 per cent for sulphur dioxide and at least 75 per cent for nitrogen oxides.

The easiest way of cleaning oil- and coal-fired power stations is to fit filters to the chimneys. The most popular types are called 'scrubbers', or Flue Gas Desulphurization Plant (FGD for short). These can reduce sulphur emissions by up to 85 per cent without seriously affecting the efficiency of the station. Several European countries already have legislation which means that all new power stations must be built with FGD, and in the Netherlands and West Germany in particular a strong effort in being made to ensure that all existing plants have them fitted too. The USA is also encouraging the fitting of FGD to many older power stations.

In the long term, it is possible that more efficient combustion technologies will be developed to burn fossil fuels in a much cleaner way without the need for extras like FGD. At present, however, they are the best solution available. Another strategy for reducing sulphur emissions would be to use coals with a lower sulphur content in power stations whose emissions are likely to end up in environmentally sensitive areas.

For cars, the simplest and most effective solution is to fit filters to the exhaust systems. Catalytic converters can eliminate up to 90 per cent of the harmful gases emitted by cars. They are already in use on one-third of the world's cars. In West Germany, people who buy cars with converters are exempt from road taxes. This kind of financial incentive scheme run by governments can contribute significantly to the speed at which consumers accept new technology. In the future, we may see the development of car engines that not only produce less pollution but burn fuel more efficiently too.

In addition to technological advances, there may be changes in the way that society organizes its use of polluting energy resources. Better public transport systems would reduce the number of cars on the roads, and lower speed limits would both help to prevent accidents and contribute to the reduction of exhaust emissions.

The power station at Didcot, Oxfordshire. It is one of Britain's twelve largest coal-fired power stations. The government has no plans to fit sulphur-scrubbing equipment to the flue (the chimney in the centre), despite pressure from environmentalists.

Projected global temperature rises

Increase in pollution (0–16 °C, 1980–2075)

Present levels of pollution (0–16 °C, 1980–2075)

Modest control of pollution (0–9 °C, 1980–2075)

Considerable slowing up in rate of pollution (0–9 °C, 1980–2075)

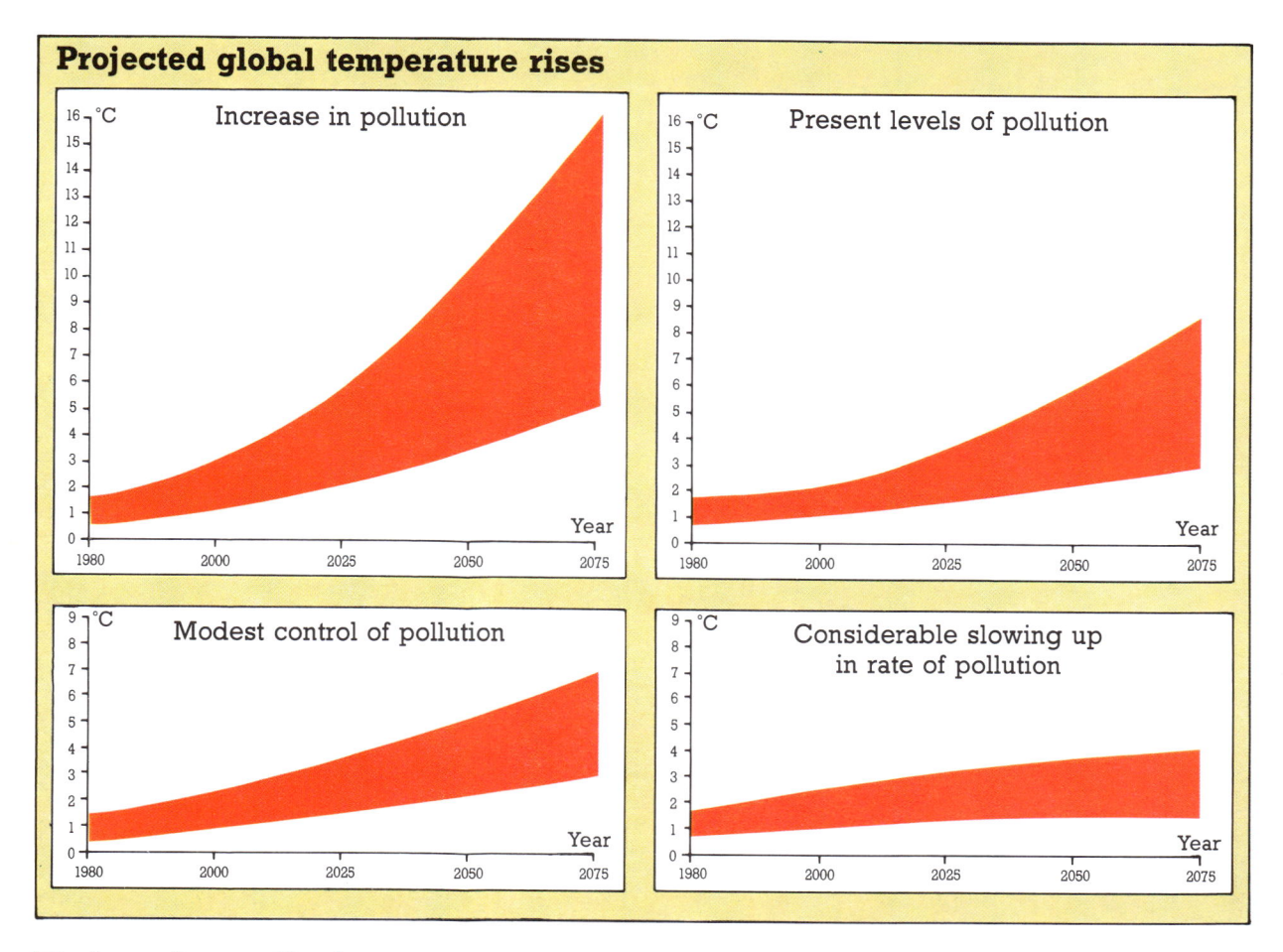

The 'greenhouse effect'

Even if ways are found, through a combination of all these measures, to reduce the problems associated with acid rain, other air pollution problems still threaten the environment. One of these is the build up of carbon dioxide in the atmosphere caused by burning fossil fuels. Carbon dioxide allows radiation from the sun to reach the earth, but prevents heat from escaping. The more the carbon dioxide builds up, the warmer the world will become. This is known as the 'greenhouse effect'.

The greenhouse effect is increased by the destruction of the tropical rain forests. Carbon dioxide is absorbed by trees and other plants in the process of photosynthesis. Rain forests represent the greatest concentration of plants in the world, so, if they are destroyed, then the concentration of carbon dioxide in the atmosphere will increase.

The graphs show predictions of the amount by which average temperatures will rise, within a range of possible levels of pollution.

It is predicted that the planet is likely to experience more warming over the next century than over the previous 10,000 years. A change in temperature of just two or three degrees could have far-reaching effects on climate, agriculture and coastal cities. A temperature increase would cause some melting of the polar ice caps which would raise the sea level by several centimetres. As a result, many coastal towns would need to erect flood barriers, and ocean currents, such as the Gulf Stream, might change their courses.

Chief among the predicted effects of global warming on agriculture is that the major corn-producing areas of the world, in North America, Asia and Africa, are likely to get less rainfall and, therefore, become less productive. It will not be so easy to build up stores of grain as a safeguard against poor harvests and inevitably it will be the developing nations who suffer most. Some climatologists believe that the present drought in Africa is the first manifestation of changes in weather patterns. Millions of people's lives could depend on the global temperature not increasing by more than about another half degree. These people, most of them living in sub-Saharan Africa, use about one per cent of the energy used by people living in the industrialized countries, but they have the misfortune to live in a more sensitive environment where they may pay with their lives for the convenience of societies which can afford to waste energy.

The ozone layer

The stratospheric ozone layer is in danger of being broken down by chlorofluorocarbons, the chemicals which are used as propellants in aerosol cans. The ozone layer protects the earth from the sun's harmful ultra-violet radiation, and its destruction would increase the danger of skin cancers. Although chlorofluorocarbons in aerosols have now been banned in the USA, and alternatives have been found, they are still in use in many European countries. There is no significant mixing between the stratospheric ozone layer and low-level ozone and so an increase in exhaust pollution does not compensate for the destruction in the stratosphere.

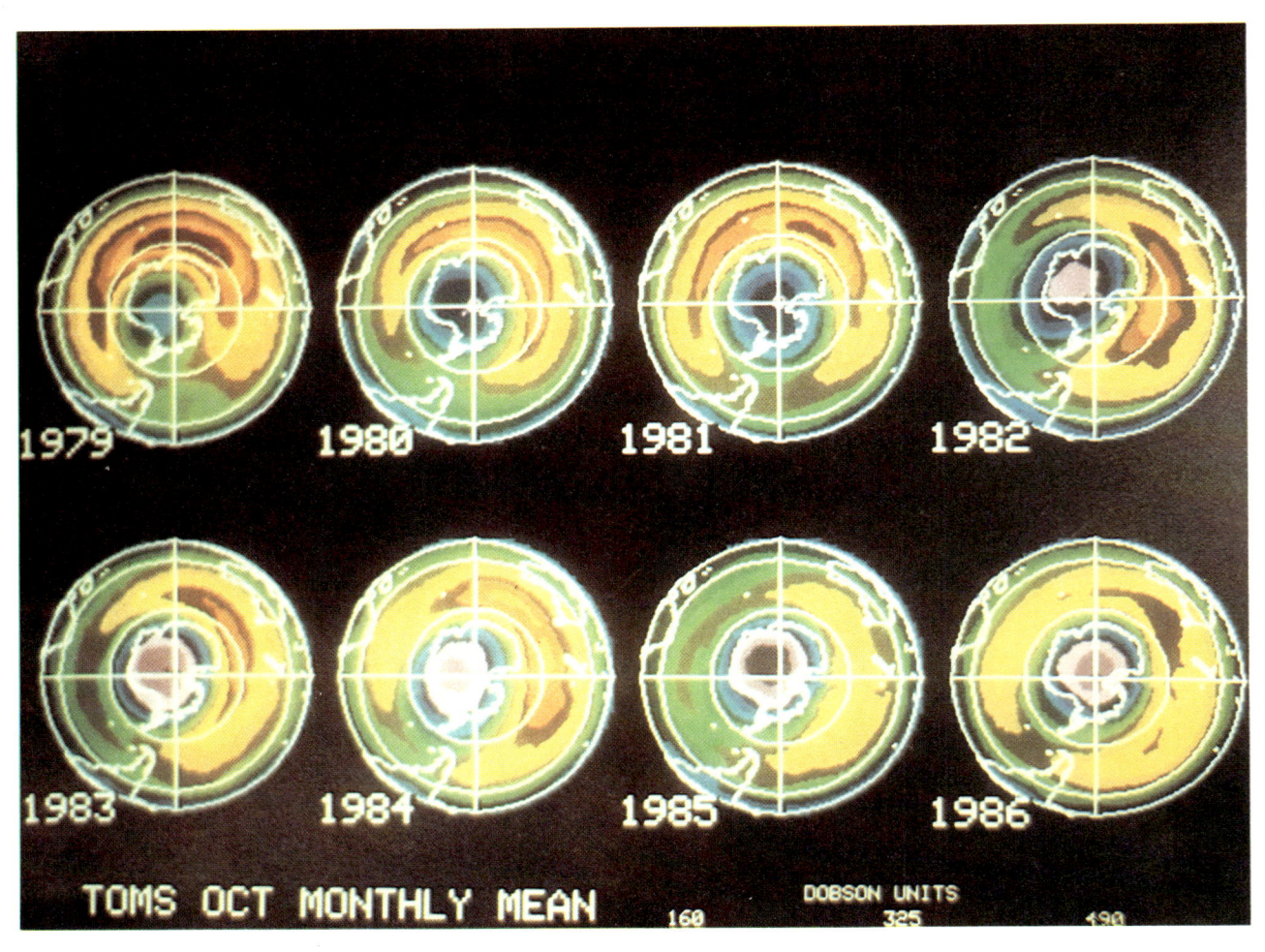

A satellite picture of the earth from above the South Pole. The growing purple patch indicates the development of a hole in the stratospheric ozone layer caused by a build-up of chlorofluorocarbons in the atmosphere.

4 The changing wilderness

No habitat on earth is as rich as a tropical rain forest. Thousands of years ago much of the earth's surface was covered in rain forest, but since then the climate has cooled and the forests are now restricted to small areas in tropical countries. They are some of the world's surviving true wilderness.

The United Nations has estimated that more than half of the world's tropical forests has disappeared since 1950. According to the American National Academy of Sciences, rain forests are being destroyed at the rate of forty hectares a minute, or 20 million hectares a year. In other words, an area of tropical forest more than nine times the size of Wales is disappearing every twelve months. At this rate, there will be none left by the year 2000 except in Central Africa and the western Brazilian Amazon. At present, forests cover some 7 per cent of the earth's land surface; 58 per cent of this is in Latin America.

The variety of life in tropical rain forests is greater than in any other place. There are as many plant species in the tropical forests of Panama, for instance, as in the whole of Europe. Malaysian forests contain more than 7,900 species of flowering plant, compared with Britain's total of 1,430 species in twice the area. Thousands of species of animal and plant almost certainly remain to be discovered and yet species are becoming extinct at a rate of about one a day. Many of them will be extinct before they have even become known to humankind.

The rain forests are also valuable because they act as a 'green lung'. In producing vast quantities of oxygen and using up carbon dioxide during photosynhesis, the tropical forests play a vital part in maintaining the balance of our atmosphere.

Areas of tropical rain forest are shrinking each year. It is estimated that there will be no undamaged forest at all by 2070.

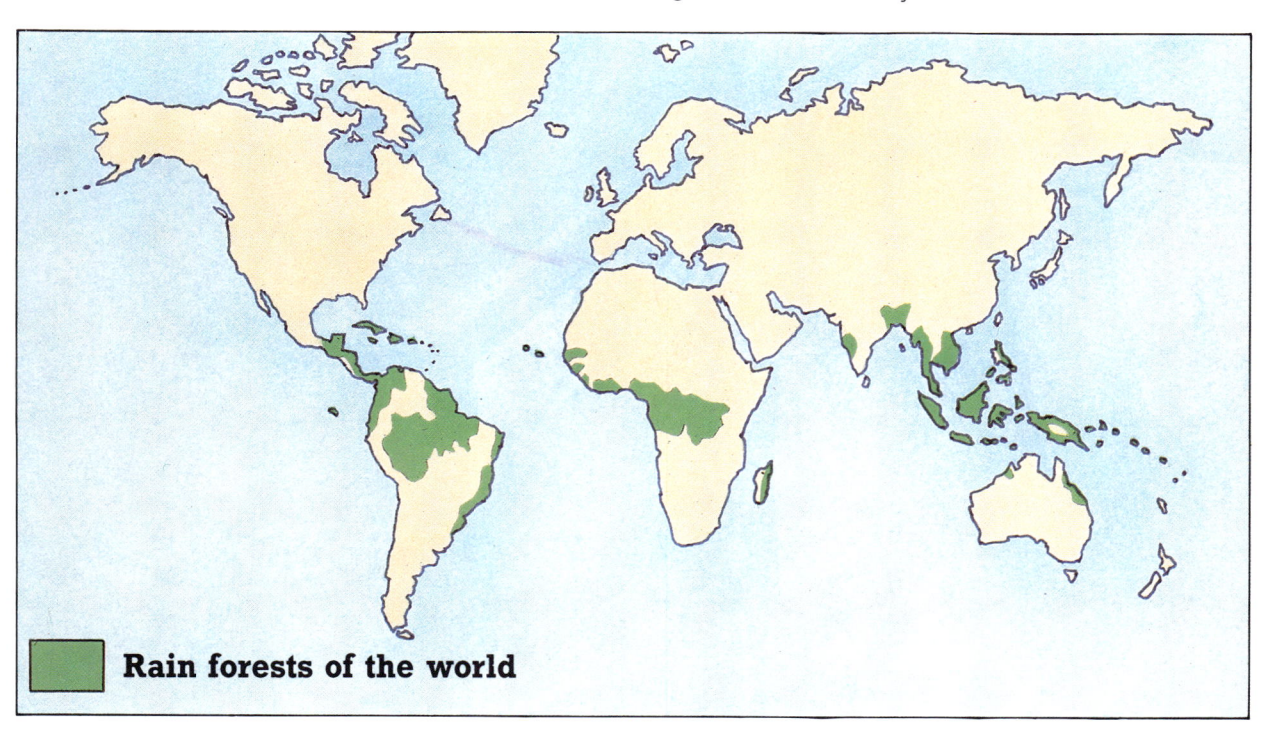

Rain forests of the world

Apart from the loss of plants and animals, there is a terrible human tragedy taking place. The destruction of the forests in over 70 countries is disastrous for the millions of indigenous people. In Brazil, for example, the Indian population has been falling by 2 million a year since 1500. These people know the forests intimately. Over centuries, they have learned about the properties of plant extracts, roots and fruits. The loss of these indigenous cultures means the loss of a vast store of knowledge about the tropical forest environment.

Disappearing forests

But what are the causes of this destruction? There are several, but the most effective is the demand from the developed countries for tropical hardwoods such as mahogany, teak and

It is likely that the settlers who are clearing the Amazonian rain forest will only stay for a few years. The soil will become eroded or exhausted and they will be forced to move on and clear a new area of forest.

rattan. Debt-ridden governments are only too happy to attract the hard currency that comes with logging operations.

The roads built by loggers open up the once impenetrable and inhospitable environment to colonization by peasants who practise shifting agriculture. They clear the land by slash and burn techniques, farm it for as long as the poor soils are productive and then move on. Many of the peasants involved in slash and burn have been expelled from their own lands. Most of the good farmland in Brazil is owned by a few very rich families. If this land was distributed more equally, the peasants would not need to move into the forest areas. It is this widening gap between the rich and poor in countries like Brazil that puts the greatest pressure on scarce and vulnerable resources.

Many of the people who settle in the forests come from coastal areas and they are not immune to the bacteria of the forest. Some, particularly the children, become ill and die.

Virtually the entire continent (of Africa) . . . is caught in a dangerous cycle of rapid population growth, inability to afford technological advances in farming, expansion of agriculture on to marginal and sensitive lands, severe deforestation and erosion, declining agricultural productivity and, too often, misguided agricultural policies.

International environmental report, World Resources 1986

The expanding deserts

As the tropical rain forests of the world shrink rapidly, the other great wilderness, the Sahara Desert, grows. It is the people of the African countries south of the Sahara who face the worst problems. This region, known as the Sahel zone, is a low-rainfall belt where the soils are extremely poor. Over thousands of years, the people of this area had developed a system of semi-nomadic cultivation which allowed the land to lie fallow and recover between periods of use. This system was uniquely suited to their harsh environment. However, the pressures of an increasing population and poor advice from agricultural aid workers have changed all this.

As more and more people are forced to eke out an existence in these marginal lands, the fields are no longer left to lie fallow. Not enough fertilizer is available and irrigation systems are inadequate to support repeated farming and grazing of the same plots of land. As a result the land is quickly degraded, the exhausted topsoils turn to dust and are blown away, and the desert advances. In some areas, the southern edge of the Sahara is rolling forward at a rate of 10km a year. For instance, ten years ago there were still acacia trees to be found 100km north of Khartoum in the Sudan. Since

A farmer in Malawi has to transfer water by hand from the main irrigation ditch into his field.

then the Sahara has crept southwards and today the city is surrounded by desert with hardly a tree to be seen for miles.

The problems caused by population growth have increased here because large areas of the most fertile land are used to grow cash crops for export rather than subsistence crops, like millet, for the local population. Cash crops are a source of foreign exchange for governments which are deeply in debt, but the change of land use has left many people on the brink of starvation.

The same problems are occurring in other parts of the works. In Mongolia, for instance, peasant farmers are struggling to hold back the dunes from their dwindling sheep-grazing lands. In parts of India, such as Karnataka or Maharashtra, the combination of prolonged drought and poor land management is causing patches of desert to form far away from any desert edge. Once patches have developed they spread, join up, and eventually form a new desert.

A Nigerian boy harvesting vegetables. Even in these arid conditions it is possible to grow a decent crop.

The key to preventing this kind of desertification is soil conservation. If areas are deforested, as in India, the micro-climate changes and moisture escapes. The soil dries out and, not being bound by the roots of trees, is easily blown away. Heavy rains wash hundreds of thousands of tonnes of valuable top soil into India's rivers every monsoon season. To make matters worse, many development aid projects have hastened the environmental decline by causing natural water tables to be lowered. Planting Eucalyptus trees (originally from Australia) in parts of Karnataka has totally destabilized the water cycle, as these trees suck water up in huge quantities.

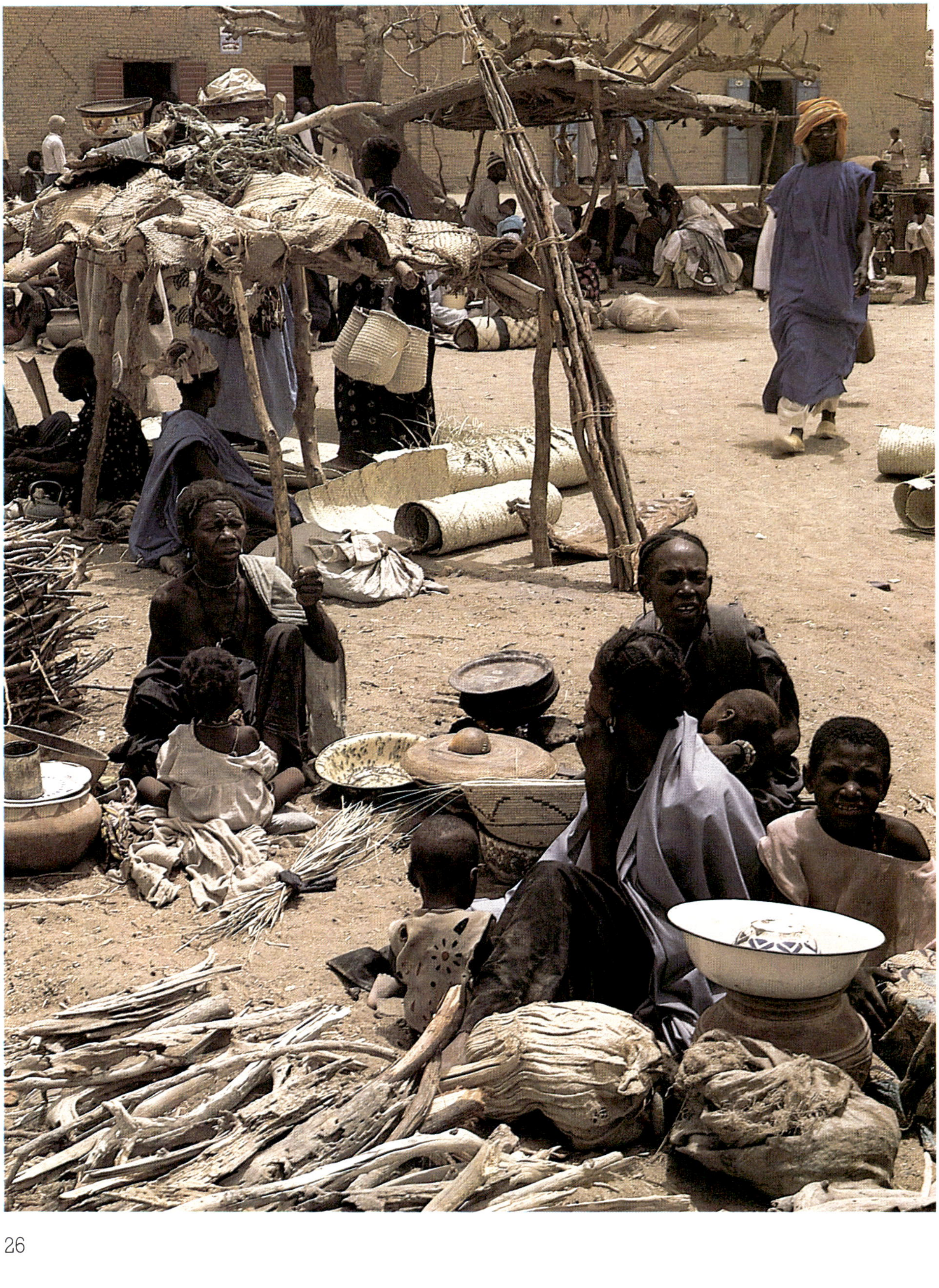

Left: People in the Sahel region collect fuel wood and sell it in the market.

Wetlands

While environmental attention has often been focused on the disappearing tropical rain forests and desertification, little heed has been paid to the crisis facing wetlands. Ranging from peat bogs and mires, to marshes and swamps, wetlands represent some of the most productive habitats on earth. Indeed, the floodplains of Indo-China and Egypt, amongst others, have supported human civilizations for thousands of years. Yet these wetlands are threatened all over the globe, with pollution, drainage, development and over-exploitation of living resources such as fish.

Wetlands are often seen as wasted land that should be turned to better use for agricultural or industrial development. In fact, they play an important part in protecting inland areas from flooding, and prevent soil that has been washed down rivers, from being lost in the oceans. The roots of plants in marshes and other coastal

Areas like this wetland in Florida are being drained and reclaimed for farming.

settlements trap the particles of soil and silt, helping to build new land and to create a fertile, productive habitat. Some wetlands are said to be able to produce up to eight times as much plant matter as a wheat field.

According to the International Union for the Conservation of Nature, large human populations are threatened by drainage schemes and dam developments. Dams on rivers above productive wetlands prevent silts and nutrients reaching the estuaries. 100,000 semi-nomadic fishermen are said to be in danger from a series of dams planned for the River Niger.

In Sudan, the giant Jonglei Canal will completely disrupt a wetland that supports some 750,000 cattle. It will also provide a haven for parasites such as those causing the terrible African disease, Schistosomiasis. The parasites are carried in snails, many of which die in the dry season, thus controlling the disease. With the building of the canal, a wet breeding site will be available the whole year round.

The Shoebill stork is one of the species threatened by the proposed Jonglei Canal in the Sudan.

Endangered species in Sudan, like the Shoebill stork and the Tiong antelope, along with hippopotami, elephant and gazelle, will be threatened by the canal.

Other wetlands are threatened, too. In Ireland, peat-cutting is causing the destruction of some of the Northern Hemisphere's most biologically important bogs. In South East Asia mangrove swamps are disappearing due to

Peat cutting, if done to excess, can threaten the ecological balance of the wetland areas of Ireland.

conversion to rice paddies and the felling of trees for wood chippings. In addition, coastal development is putting vital feeding and wintering sites for migratory birds of North America and Europe in danger.

5 Seas at risk

Two-thirds of the earth's surface is covered by water. These vast areas of ocean have always fascinated humankind; they have inspired myths and attracted numerous adventurers. The sea has also offered a seemingly inexhaustible supply of food in the form of fish, shellfish, whales and seaweed.

The enormous size of the oceans has led generations of people to think that they could use them as bottomless dustbins and catch any amount of fish without causing permament damage. However, the marine environment, like any other resource, must be used sensibly. There is no reason why the oceans should not continue to produce a bountiful supply of food for millenia to come, but only if we treat them with respect. Recently, overfishing on a global scale, the hunting of the great whales and waste disposal have begun to take their toll.

Overfishing

The increasing hunger of the world's population for protein-rich food has led to small, local fishing fleets being replaced by enormous factory ships that fish the seas from pole to pole and can stay at sea for years if necessary. As a result, the fish population is hounded through the oceans, leaving almost nowhere for it to recover undisturbed. For this reason, bitter political battles have been fought over fishing rights as nations try to protect their own fish stocks from other fishing fleets.

In the deep seas, however, away from any territorial waters, anything goes. Japanese fishermen in the Pacific, for instance, use giant drift nets – so-called because they are released from ships into the ocean currents, allowed to drift for hundreds of kilometres, and then hauled back on board. On the way, the nets pick up virtually everything in their path, regardless of edibility or utility. Most distressing are the numbers of dolphins, porpoises, whales and turtles that die in the nets every year. Worse still, many of the nets are never recovered, but are left to float on the currents for years, reaping a deadly harvest.

A Russian 'Klondyker' which processes and freezes fish, storing it for months.

Despite the ban, some countries continue to kill whales and endanger the species.

Fishing quotas

Governments are being forced to find ways of halting the uncontrolled rape of the oceans' resources. One, so far only moderately successful, tactic has been to set fishing quotas. This means that only a certain weight of particular types of fish can be taken by any one country's fishing fleet in one year. This kind of regulation has been applied to cod and herring in the North Sea, and to anchovies in the Pacific. Unfortunately, fishing quotas are only as strong as the will with which they are enforced.

One of the most successful campaigns to preserve marine species has been the protection of whales. Intense public pressure in the 1970s, largely fuelled by publicity given to the appalling, bloody slaughter of whales by Japanese, Russian and Norwegian harpoon ship fleets, brought about international action. The campaign was led by organizations like the World Wildlife Fund, Friends of the Earth and Greenpeace. Through the supra-national body of the International Whaling Commission (IWC), a moratorium on whaling was declared in the early 1980s. There is only one loophole which allows some whales to be caught for 'scientific purposes', and their meat to be sold afterwards.

Waste disposal

Apart from overfishing, the greatest threat to the seas is posed by pollution. The most famous, and one of the earliest, serious pollution incidents that affected humans was the Minemata disaster of 1953. At Minemata Bay in Japan, cats were observed staggering around, hundreds of dead fish were found on the beach, and crows and dogs that ate the fish died. By December, a local person had developed the same symptoms as the cats – loss of coordination, partial blindness, numb limbs and then convulsions leading to coma and death. By the end of 1956, there had been more than seventy-five cases of Minemata Disease, as it came to be called; eighteen of these were infants. The cause was found to be the exceptionally high levels of mercury in fish and shellfish eaten by people around the bay. The source of the mercury was a factory manufacturing plastics and discharging contaminated effluent straight into the sea.

Since then, much more care has been taken about the chemicals that are piped directly into the sea and most industrialized nations have strict laws governing the discharge of liquid waste. This of course does not prevent some

The dead cormorant in the foreground of this picture has been killed by the oil covering this Humberside beach which the men in special vehicles are attempting to clean.

companies from trying to cut corners and escape detection. Problems of this sort are prevalent in the developing countries and many cases of pollution-related disease have been recorded in recent years in countries such as Malaysia, Thailand and Vietnam, where many people rely on a diet of fish from highly polluted coastal areas.

The North Sea

If the Pacific has a problem with overfishing and the heavy metal pollution from factories, then the North Sea, between Britain, Scandinavia and continental Europe, has pollution problems of a far more insidious kind. The North Sea is largely surrounded by land. This

Industrial waste in the Rhine near Düsseldorf in West Germany.

means that it takes a long time to exchange all the water in it. It is one of the most productive seas in the world in terms of fish, but it is fast becoming one of the most polluted.

Four of the dirtiest rivers in the Northern Hemisphere flow into the North Sea: the Rhine, the Elbe, the Thames and the Humber. The Rhine and Elbe carry the effluent from the industries and cities of Europe's most industrialized countries. The rivers bring metals, human sewage, pesticides, fertilizer washed off agricultural land, detergents and a host of less familiar substances such as PCBs and phenol. PCBs are toxic chemicals used in transformers and in making plastics.

A particularly serious discharge of waste occurred in November 1986, when a fire at the Sandoz chemical factory on the Swiss part of the Rhine caused a spill of tonnes of toxic liquids into the river. The stream of pesticides, solvents and heavy metals flowed through West Germany and the Netherlands, killing millions of fish and threatening water supplies, before finally ending up in the North Sea. We can only hope that this disaster has taught us lessons about the hazards of chemical storage which will prevent any similar accidents in the future.

The Sandoz disaster, however, was not the only contributor to the unhealthy state of the North Sea. Incineration of toxic waste at sea, the discharge of raw sewage, lead pollution from car exhaust fumes, nitrates and phosphates from agricultural run-off, and oil pollution from ships and rigs, are just some of the other causes for concern.

With so many pollutants entering the marine environment, it is difficult to tell exactly what effects the different toxic chemicals have on sea life. A greatly strengthened research effort by the Dutch and West German authorities over the last ten years, has begun to indicate the ecological problems caused by pollution.

Most frightening perhaps is the effect of the 'toxic chemical soup' on fish in the North Sea. New diseases are being discovered in fish like dab and flounder, such as skin sores and viral infections. Worst of all is the rise in the number of cancers that fish are developing. In some parts of the North Sea as many as 40 per cent of adult flounders have liver cancers. Scientists point to pollution as the only possible cause.

In 1986 Dutch researchers published results that showed a firm relationship between water pollution and high infant mortality in seals. There was a high incidence of dead or deformed young seals where they had been exposed to PCBs in the North Sea.

The build-up of nutrients, from fertilizers, sewage and air pollution, is another serious concern. These are mostly nitrogen compounds, which upset the balance of life in the sea. The nitrates and phosphates act like fertilizer in the sea, but they encourage the fast growth of marine algae, rather than crops! The algae, with a very short seasonal life-cycle, bloom, forming so-called red or brown tides, and then die. When they die, they decompose

Men wearing protective clothing while clearing up the toxic waste left by the fire at the Sandoz warehouse.

near the sea bed, using up most of the dissolved oxygen in the water in the process. The lack of oxygen can kill off almost all the fish in the immediate area. This problem is worst in shallow areas off the Danish, West German and Dutch coasts which are a vital nursery area for millions of young fish. This process of eutrophication could therefore be a threat to the productivity of the whole region.

Taking action

The state of the North Sea is of such great concern to the eight surrounding countries that their governments met to discuss the problem in 1984. A second inter-governmental meeting on the North Sea was organized in 1987 in London. The results of these meetings illustrate the two different approaches which can be taken towards pollution control.

The British Government took the view that more research needs to be done in order to

The effects of pollution in the North Sea are passed on, through the fish they eat, to the seabirds that live there.

assess the problems fully. They believe that a direct link between specific pollutants and their effects must be demonstrated before action can be justified. On the other hand, countries such as the Netherlands and West Germany promote what is known as the 'anticipation principle'. In essence, this is a 'better safe than sorry' approach which favours prompt action whenever there are strong indications that a problem is looming.

The conflict over which environmental policy is the best one for the North Sea has not yet been resolved. It is just one of the many debates about the best way to deal with environmental problems. Similar discussions are under way in areas as diverse as international air pollution legislation, countryside conservation and developmental aid policies.

6 Working for the environment

In the last three chapters, we have looked at some of the world's most pressing environmental problems and seen examples of solutions to these problems. There are technological solutions, such as FGD for power stations and catalytic converters for cars; social solutions, such as better transport systems and land redistribution; and management solutions, such as conserving fish stocks and disposing of waste products safely. The implementation of all these measures depends on political will and there is still a long way to go before they are adopted internationally.

The cost of environmental protection

In most debates about environmental policies, the cost of implementing a particular solution is weighed against the benefits of that solution. This is known as cost/benefit analysis. Politicians want to be certain that the measures they take to combat environmental problems will not bankrupt their country. Conservationists, on the other hand, often call for solutions which are too expensive, or not technically feasible. Some kind of compromise must be reached which protects the environment, but does not cause undue strain on the government's economic resources.

In Britain, such a compromise is known as the Best Practicable Environmental Option, or BPEO. It is arrived at after considering all the different options, seeing how effective each will be in helping to alleviate problems and how much they cost. After applying this procedure to the problem of reducing nitrogen oxide emissions from power stations, the British Government announced in the spring of 1987 that it would fit new boiler systems to the twelve dirtiest stations. These boilers reduce polluting gas emissions by only about 30 per cent, but they are more than fifteen times cheaper than catalytic systems which can reduce pollution by 80 per cent. The catalytic systems are being used in West German and Japan.

In making decisions that take account of cost, it is also necessary to try to work out the cost of *not* doing anything at all. For instance, it may seem costly to European motor manufacturers and petrol companies to adapt to using unleaded petrol, but since lead in car exhaust fumes is thought to be damaging to children's health, the change might lead to long-term savings on health spending. In the USA, all petrol is now lead-free.

Nuclear waste being dumped at sea. Many people feel that this is unsafe and will create enormous problems of pollution in the future.

Lemurs, which exist only in Madagascar, are endangered because of the destruction of the forest there.

The direct cost of not doing anything about acid rain will be to the forestry, fishing and tourism industries of the industrialized countries. Added costs, which are less easy to calculate, could be to health services and to the authorities responsible for repairing buildings damaged by air pollution.

Many countries, including Britain, have adopted a policy called the 'Polluter Pays Principle'. This principle dictates that those industries responsible for polluting the environment, should pay the cost of cleaning up afterwards. The idea is that companies will find it cheaper to emit less pollution in the first place, rather than pay for a restoration operation. In practice, unfortunately, the Polluter Pays Principle is seldom strictly enforced, and the estimates of the damage caused are usually far too small.

In the long term, the cheapest way of dealing with environmental problems is likely to be to prevent them reaching a critical stage in the first place. However, the cost of taking no action cannot be measured only in monetary terms. It also affects the quality of our surrounding. Do we want to see our most beautiful monuments crumble away, or to live in a country devoid of trees? Does it matter if we cause the extinction of animals and plants by destroying their habitats? And are we content to damage our own health and the health of future generations?

These are all considerations the value of which cannot be assessed objectively and so, as long as policies are formulated on the basis of cost, they are all too easily ignored.

The environment and development

The environmental crisis is closely connected to the international trading system, which works against developing countries, the debt crisis and the arms trade. An international plan for action is essential but it must take into account the growing gap between the economies of the industrialized and the developing countries. We have seen examples in sub-Saharan Africa and the Amazon rain forests of how some of the world's poorest people are forced to degrade their environment in order to survive. This also applies to the governments of developing countries who need the money

Mrs Gro Harlem Brundtland, the leader of the World Commission on Environment and Development, talking to reporters.

created by cash crops and logging operations to pay the interest on their debts to foreign banks and to pay for development programmes. With pressure from the current arms race, they often spend large amounts of money on defence, thus doing critical damage to their own development efforts.

In order to address these problems and others, the World Commission on Environment and Development was set up in 1984 under the leadership of Mrs Gro Harlem Brundtland of Norway. Nine hundred days later – a period in which an estimated 60 million people died of diseases related to malnutrition and unsafe drinking water, and during which the Chernobyl, Bhopal and Sandoz disasters occurred – the Commission published its conclusions.

The Commission's report, *Our Common Future – From One Earth to One World*, is one of the most important documents of the decade. It reviews the threats which current patterns of development present to global society. Many of the things which the report highlights have been said by environmentalists before, but the authority of the Brundtland Commission and the comprehensiveness of the report give a new perspective. Most important of all, it is not a scaremongering report, laden with doom and gloom; it offers a way forward for humankind.

Nevertheless, the catalogue of environmental mismanagement to be found in the report is quite chilling. Some of the figures used to describe the global environmental crises are almost incomprehensible. Economic activity has multiplied to create a $13 trillion world economy. Industrial production has grown fiftyfold in the last century. Every year another 6 million hectares of productive dryland turns to desert and 11 million hectares of forest is destroyed. Every year during the 1970s more than 24 million people suffered from drought and more than 15 million became flood victims.

International cooperation

The Brundtland report, however, points out that with a determined effort by governments we could move towards a new, sustainable economy. Such a change will depend on all decisions about technology and the exploitation of resources being made with regard to future as well as present needs. This means that the problem of finding solutions to the great global crises, economic, developmental and environmental alike, is one of political will. International cooperation is vital. We must realize that we are all part of one world and must start to behave accordingly. It is international cooperation which has been lacking in the past. There can be no doubt, though, that as we move towards the end of the 1980s, a time dubbed by some 'the decade of destruction', a greater willingness to work together on issues of global environmental importance is emerging.

Through various international forums like the United Nations, the EEC (European Economic Community), and the International Tropical Timber Organization, countries are working towards agreeing measures to protect species, habitats and indigenous peoples. A variety of international legislation exists: the Ramsar Convention to protect wetlands, the Geneva Convention on Air Pollution, the International Whaling Commission and the Convention on International Trade in Endangered Species (CITES), are just a few. Some are more successful than others, but with every new convention, comes a new lesson to be learned.

As public awareness of environmental topics throughout the world is raised, so governments become more willing to act. The issues of acid rain and nuclear power have galvanized public interest in Europe. In West Germany, Norway and Switzerland, the environment now ranks above employment or housing as a political issue. Raising the environment issue on the political agenda is a slow process in the USA and the UK, but it has spawned the 'green' political parties. In West Germany *Die Grünen* now has more than 12 per cent of the vote, and is a highly significant factor in the country's politics.

Conservation

Throughout the previous chapters, we have talked of the environment and of environmental protection, but scarcely of conservation. The principle underlying environmental protection,

HRH Prince Charles (left) chatting to two British Civil Servants before the Conference on the Protection of the North Sea, held in London in November 1987. In his speech at the Conference the Prince criticized the British Government for not acting quickly enough to control pollution.

must always be conservation. Not just of species and of habitats, but of resources as well. For example, by conserving energy in the home and industry, we not only reduce energy bills, but also slow the rate at which pollutants like carbon dioxide and sulphur dioxide, generated from fossil-fuel power stations, are emitted.

Careful use of living and non-living resources is the key to conservation. Conservation of coal and oil for future generations, conservation of species for people to see, and wild places to see them in.

This Commission believes that people can build a future that is more prosperous, more just and more secure. Our report is not a prediction of ever increasing environmental decay, poverty and hardship in an ever more polluted world among ever decreasing resources. We see instead the possibility for a new era of economic growth, one that must be based on policies that sustain and expand the environmental resource base. And we believe such growth to be absolutely essential to relieve the great poverty that is deepening in much of the developing world.

One Common Future – From one Earth to One World.
The Brundtland Commission report 1987.

7 What can I do?

Edmund Burke once said: 'Nobody made a greater mistake than he who did nothing because he could do only a little.' This, in a nutshell, is the philosophy behind the environmental movement. Environmentalists, conservationists, 'greens', call them what you will, are attempting to slow the trend of environmental degradation by every legal method. They lobby governments to introduce legislation and join international agreements; they conduct and commission research and analyze the results of others; they monitor the activities of farmers and industries; and they demonstrate and take legal action against polluters and unscrupulous developers. They also work hard to influence public opinion, the strength of which cannot be overestimated.

Listening to public opinion is the essence of a democratic society. Even without environmental organizations, people would find a voice to protest about the destruction of the wilderness, air pollution or the state of inner cities. Each one of us is an environmentalist in our own way. We may care about the lack of public transport in our town or to our village, we may worry over the noise and smoke from trucks on the roads, or we may pursue a recreation, such as sailing, fishing or bird-watching, which

Protesters in Plogoff in France, demonstrating against a proposed nuclear power station.

depends on the natural world.

It is a short step from worrying about local problems such as litter in the streets or vehicle exhausts to being concerned about the wider issues at national and international level. In making this step, the link is drawn between individual responsibility and collective responsibility. If we believe there should be less litter, then we make our own contribution by being careful not to drop things on the ground. Likewise, if we are concerned about the destruction of the rain forests, we can make sure that we do not use tropical hardwoods like teak or mahogany ourselves. Hardwoods are used for all sorts of things, from plywood to window frames, veneer and furniture.

The harmful gases in the exhaust fumes of a car can be reduced by 90 per cent if a catalytic converter is fitted. Lead-free petrol also helps to reduce the damage caused by fumes.

Refusing to buy certain products – a consumer boycott – because their manufacture or their use is environmentally damaging in some way, can have successful results. An international consumer boycott of whale products was instrumental in a trade ban being imposed on them in Europe in 1982. In the late 1970s, a consumer campaign against aerosols in the USA led to a ban on the use of chlorofluorocarbons as propellants. Although these chemicals are still legal in some European countries many people do not buy aerosol cans as a protest. After all, there are perfectly acceptable alternatives available. This also applies to other everyday items. For example, fly sprays, weed-killers and slug pellets contain dangerous pesticides and are usually available in less harmful forms.

In our everyday lives we can also take care of our environment. Using less detergent for washing clothes and dishes prevents damaging

There are many groups who campaign against the pollution of the environment. These members of Greenpeace are protesting against pollution in the North Sea.

phosphates from reaching rivers and lakes. Electricity and water, for example, are used enormously wastefully throughout the industrialized world. It is easy to think of a dozen ways of reducing electricity consumption, from the flick of a switch in an unoccupied room to the more comprehensive solution of improving the energy conservation potential of a house through draughtproofing and insulation.

Apart from changes in our daily habits, we can start to use our power as democrats by writing to our elected representatives. The influence of a personal letter to a politician should never be underestimated. Just five or six letters on a particular issue, say wildlife conservation or oil pollution, can be enough to start a ball rolling.

The status of the environment as a political issue varies from country to country. In West Germany and Scandinavia, it has risen over the last few years to a high position on the political agenda. The German Green Party even has a substantial number of seats in the national and European Parliaments. In Britain, on the other hand, environmental issues hardly rated a mention in the general election campaign of 1987.

There are many ways in which we can make ourselves part of the growing public movement working towards a sustainable future. We can join environmental organizations at local level which concern themselves with both local and global issues, and publish informative magazines for their supporters. We can also contribute through our own lifestyle and through political representation. In some cases it is enough just to keep ourselves informed so that we can argue the case for the environment with our contemporaries.

No one should forget that the earth's resources are limited and that we do have the ability and means to prevent their total depletion. This depends not merely on politicians, but on people like you, who every day in a hundred ways interact with your environment. Remember the slogan 'think globally – act locally' and you will be recognizing the same truth as the philosopher Theodor Roszak when he said: 'The needs of the planet and the needs of the person have become one.'

Glossary

Acid rain In its strict sense, this is acidic deposition in a wet or dry form, generally as a result of reactions involving sulphur or nitrogen gases in the atmosphere. Acid rain is often used to describe the whole problem of air pollution causing damage to the environment.

Climatologist A scientist who studies weather patterns, and who predicts, on the basis of historical information and computer modelling, what future trends may be.

Conservation The protection, preservation and careful management of natural resources and the environment.

Chain reaction A self-perpetuating reaction, where every nuclear reaction causes another.

Catalytic Converter Apparatus fitted to the exhaust pipe of a car, which reduces pollution by reactions which take place on the surface of a platinum film.

DDT A chemical called dichlorodiphenyltrichloroethane, an insecticide that builds up in the food chain and remains in the environment for a long time. It is banned in the UK and the USA but widely used still in developing countries.

Deciduous trees Ones which shed their leaves in autumn.

Ecosystem The biological term for a community of organisms and their environment.

Effluent Liquid industrial waste.

Enclosure Acts Acts of Parliament which fenced off common land.

Environmental impact analysis A study that is carried out before any major development takes place, in order to see what the consequences for the environment could be.

Indigenous Originating or occurring naturally in a country or region.

International Whaling Commission The inter-governmental body that decides how many whales, and of which species, can be hunted every year.

Kibbutz An agricultural settlement in modern Israel, owned and administered communally by its members.

Micro-climate The climate of a very small area.

Millenia Thousands of years.

Nordic Council A joint council of Ministers from Finland, Norway, Sweden and Denmark that acts as a commission to study issues of mutual interest, such as acid rain.

Nutrients Mineral substances absorbed by the roots of plants.

PCBs Polychlorinatedbiphenyls – chemicals manufactured by man that are used in transformers and which remain in the environment for a long time. They are partly responsible for declining seal populations.

Stratospheric ozone layer A thin layer of the gas ozone about 20–40km above the earth's surface, which protects us from ultra-violet rays emitted by the sun. It is slowly being destroyed by the release of chemicals used for aerosols, fridges and polystyrene manufacture.

Subsistence farming A type of farming in which most of the produce is consumed by the farmer and his or her family, leaving little or nothing to be sold at market.

Toxic Poisonous.

Yield The amount of product produced.

Books to Read

Rachel Carson, *Silent Spring* (Penguin 1965)
Catherine Caufield, *In the Rain Forest* (Picador 1985)
Susan George, *How the Other Half Dies – the Real Reason for World Hunger* (Penguin 1976)
Ian Greer, *Right to be Heard – A Guide to Political Representation and Parliamentary Procedure* (Ian Greer Associates 1985)
Angela King and Sue Clifford, *Holding Your Ground – An Action Guide to Local Conservation* (Temple Smith 1985)
Alan Miller and Irving Mintzer, *The Sky is the Limit – Strategies for Protecting the Ozone Layer* (World Resources Institute 1986)
Norman Myers (ed.), *The Gaia Atlas of Planetary Management – For today's caretakers of tomorrow's world* (Pan Books 1985)

Fred Pearce, *Acid Rain* (Penguin 1987)
Jonathon Porritt (ed.), *Friends of the Earth Handbook* (Macdonald Optima 1987)
John Seymour and Herbert Girardet, *Far from Paradise – The Story of Man's Impact on the Environment* (BBC 1986)
John Seymour and Herbert Girardet, *Blueprint for a Green Planet – How you can take practical action today to fight pollution* (Dorling Kindersley 1987)
Des Wilson, *Citizen Action – Taking Action in Your Community* (Longman 1986)
The World Commission on Environment and Development, *Our Common Future – From One Earth to One World* (OUP 1987)
The Global 2000 Report to the President (Penguin 1982)

Picture acknowledgements

Richard Baker 17; Camera Press 12; Bruce Coleman 16 (Hans Reinhard), 27 (M. Timothy O'Keefe), 29 (Chris Bonington), 35 (G. Ziesler); Greenpeace 36 (Gleizes), 43 (Geering); Frank Lane 32 (Roger Tidman); Tony Morrison 22; NASA, 20; Oxfam 24 (Jeremy Hartley), 25 (Jeremy Hartley), 26; Oxford Scientific Films, cover (P.J. DeVries); Planet Earth 30 (J. Duncan), 31 (Nigel Merrett); Popperfoto 15; Rex Features 11, 13 (Mahendra Sinh), 38; Frank Spooner, frontispiece (D. Gutekunst), 34 (D. Gutekunst); Survival Anglia 28 (Cindy Buxton), 37 (Tony Bomford); Topham 40, 41; John Wright 8, 10, 23; ZEFA 6 (E Rekos), 7, 14 (Paolo Koch), 18 (I. J. Belcher), 33 (G. Sommer), 42 (Kalter Witterung); artwork by Malcolm S. Walker.

Further information

Here are some addresses of organizations who will help you learn more about your environment and how to protect it.

Friends of the Earth
26–28 Underwood Street
London N1

Greenpeace
30 Islington Green
London N1

Council for the Preservation of Rural England
4 Hobart Place
London SW1W 0HY

World Wildlife Fund
Panda House
11–13 Ockford Road
Godalming
Surrey GU7 1QU

Royal Society for Nature Conservation
The Green,
Nettleham,
Lincoln LN2 2NR

Intermediate Technology Development Group
9 King Street
London WC2E 8HN

Marine Conservation Society
4 Gloucester Road
Ross-on-Wye
Herefordshire

Survival International
29 Craven Street
London WC2N 5NT

Oxfam
274 Banbury Road
Oxford OX2 7DZ

International Institute for Environment and Development
3 Endsleigh Street
London WC1H 0DD

Index

The numbers in **bold** refer to the pictures.

acid rain 15, 16–17, **16**, 19, 37, 39
aerosols 20, 42
agriculture 17, 19, 23, 27
arms trade 38, 39

Best Practicable Environmental Option 36
Bhopal 13, **13**, 39
Brundtland, Gro Harlem **38**, 39, 40

cadmium 13
cancer 12, 34
carbon dioxide 19, 21, 40
carbon monoxide 17
cash crops 25, 39
catalytic converters 18, 36, **42**
Chernobyl **11**, 12, **12**, 39
chlorofluorocarbons 20, 42
Clean Air Act (1956) 15, 16
climate 8, **19**
conservation 39–40, 43
Convention on International Trade in Endangered Species 39
cyclists 14, **14**

DDT 13
debt crisis 38
deforestation 25
deserts 8, 9, 24–5, **24, 25, 26**, 39
detergents 42

ecology 8
ecosystem 8
  marine 17
electricity 7, 11, 43
energy 6, 10, 20, 40
European Economic Community 39
exhaust 7, 14, 17, 18, 20, 34, **42**, 36, 42

fish 16, 30, **30**, 32, 33, 34, **35**
fishing quotas 31
Flue Gas Desulphurization Plant 18, **18**, 36
Friends of the Earth, 32

Geneva Convention on Air Pollution 39
grassland 9
'greenhouse effect' 15, 19–20
Green Party, West Germany 39, 41, 43
Greenpeace 32, **43**

hydrocarbons 17

industry 9, 13, 27
intensive farming 6, 9
International Tropical Timber Organization 39
International Union for the Conservation of Nature 28
International Whaling Commission 32, 39
irrigation, 24, **24**

Jonglei Canal 28, **28**

lead 13, 17, 34
logging 23, 39

marine algae 34
mercury 32
Minemata Bay (disease) 32

nitrates 34
nitrogen oxides 15, 16, 17, 18
nomads 9
Nordic Council 17
North Sea 35, **35, 43**
  Conference 35, **40**
nuclear waste **36**

oil pollution **32**, 34, 43
oxygen 21
ozone 17, 20

PCBs 33
pesticides 13
phosphates 34, 43
plants, extinction of 21, 37
pollution of
  air 7, 8, 10, 13, 14, **15**, 15–20, **17**
  lakes 9, 10, 16
  rivers 8, 10, 13, 16
  seas 8, 10, 13, 33, **33, 36, 43**
  soil **12**, 16

population growth 25
power
  coal 7, 11, 17, 18, **19**
  gas 11
  nuclear 7, 11–12, 39, **41**
  oil 7, 11, 17, 18
  wave 7

radiation 11–12, **11–12**
radioactive waste 11
rain forests 6, 8, **8, 10**, 14, 19, 21, **21, 22, 37**, 22–3, 38, 39, 42
Ramzar Convention 39
Rhine 34
roads 14

Sandoz, **2**, 34, **34**, 39
stratospheric ozone layer 15, 20, **20**
subsistence farming 9, 25
sulphur dioxide 15, 16, 17, 18, 40

transport 6, 13, 14
  public 41

Union Carbide 13
United Nations 17, 21, 39
unleaded petrol 36, **42**

waste disposal 30
West German Forest Survey (1983) 17
wetlands 27–9, **27, 29**
whales 8, 30, **31**, 32, 42
wildlife, extinction of 8, 9, 21, 29, 37
World Commission on Environment and Development 39, 40
World Wildlife Fund 32

47